E-Commerce Business Shopify & Dropshipping

2 Books in 1

How to Make Money Online Selling on Shopify, Amazon FBA, eBay, Facebook, Instagram and Other Social Medias

BY BRETT STANDARD

© Copyright 2019 - All rights reserved.

The contents of this book may not be reproduced, duplicated or transmitted without direct written permission from the author.

Under no circumstances will any legal responsibility or blame be held against the publisher for any reparation, damages, or monetary loss due to the information herein, either directly or indirectly.

Legal Notice:

You cannot amend, distribute, sell, use, quote or paraphrase any part of the content within this book without the consent of the author.

Disclaimer Notice:

Please note the information contained within this document is for educational and entertainment purposes only. No warranties of any kind are expressed or implied. Readers acknowledge that the author is not engaging in the rendering of legal, financial, medical or professional advice. Please consult a licensed professional before attempting any techniques outlined in this book.

By reading this document, the reader agrees that under no circumstances are the author responsible for any losses, direct or indirect, which are incurred as a result of the use of information contained within this document, including, but not limited to, —errors, omissions, or inaccuracies.

TABLE OF CONTENTS

SHOPIFY vi

INTRODUCTION VII
CHAPTER 1 - WHAT IS SHOPIFY AND HOW DOES IT WORK? 1
CHAPTER 2 - THE DIFFERENT SHOPIFY PLANS 7
CHAPTER 3 - SHOPIFY FEATURES 15
CHAPTER 4 - WHY USE SHOPIFY? 22
CHAPTER 5 - TOP SHOPIFY APPS 25
CHAPTER 6 - SETTING UP YOUR SHOPIFY STORE 34
CHAPTER 7 - ADDING YOUR PRODUCTS 38
CHAPTER 8 - DOMAINS AND EMAILS 40
CHAPTER 9 - PAGES, DESIGN AND PAYMENTS 44
CHAPTER 10 - BEFORE YOU GO LIVE 50
CHAPTER 11 - DO'S AND DON'TS 53
BONUS CHAPTER - SHOPIFY AND AMAZON 57
BONUS CHAPTER - SHOPIFY AND FACEBOOK 65
CONCLUSION 71

DROPSHIPPING 72

INTRODUCTION 73
CHAPTER 1 - HOW DOES THE DROPSHIPPING MODEL WORK? 75
  Here Is How The Dropshipping Model Works 76
CHAPTER 2 - THE ADVANTAGES OF STARTING A DROPSHIPPING BUSINESS 87
  Less Startup Capital Investment Compared To Other Models 88
  Low Overhead Costs 89
  Easy For You To Get Started 90
  Can Be Highly Scalable 91
  You Can Do It From Any Location 92
  Ensures A High Customer Lifetime Value 93
  Minimizes Your Risk 93
  Enables You To Come To Market A Lot Quicker 94
  Sell An Unlimited Selection Of Products 95
  Access To Unlimited Amounts Of Inventory 96
  Less Time Consumed 96
  Less Products With Little Risk 97
  Test Products With Little Risk 97
  Increases Your Favorability With Wholesalers 98
CHAPTER 3 - THE DISADVANTAGES OF STARTING A DROPSHIPPING BUSINESS 99
  Low-Profit Margins 100
  Suppliers Are Prone To Making Human Errors 102
  Issues With Inventory 102
  Shipping Costs Can Get Complicated 103
  Competition 103

iii

Shipping Can Be Slow 104
Lack Adequate Product Information 105
The Quality Of Customer Service Is Beyond Your Control 106
Pay Relatively High Fulfillment Costs 107
Pay-Per-Click Advertising Is Way More Expensive And Less Effective 108
Difficult To Brand Your Products 109
Little Control Over The Quality Of Your Products 109
CHAPTER 4 - HOW TO START-UP THE BUSINESS 111
   Find A Niche 111
   Find Suppliers 112
   Find A Product 113
   Form A Business 114
   Get Permits And Licenses 115
   Choose A Sales Platform 115
   Create A Payment System 116
   Set Up A Customer Service System 117
   Create A List Of Offerings 117
   Buy The Product From The Supplier Whenever You Make A Sale 118
   Find Ways To Market Your Business 119
CHAPTER 5 - NICHE AND PRODUCT SELECTION 120
   Know The Difference Between Trending And Evergreen Niches 121
   Finding A Niche Using Google Trends 122
   Finding A Niche Using Facebook 123
   Finding A Niche Using Trend Hunter 124
   Finding A Niche Using Instagram 124
   Finding A Niche Using Aliexpress 125
   Finding A Niche Using Amazon Tools 126
   Other Ways To Find A Niche 126
   Researching Your Competitors 128
CHAPTER 6 - HOW DOES THE SUPPLY CHAIN AND FULFILLMENT PROCESS WORK? 129
   Manufacturers 130
   Wholesalers Or Suppliers 131
   Retailers And Dropshippers 131
   Order Placement By The Customer With Your Business 133
   Order Placement By Your Business With The Supplier 134
   The Supplier Ships The Order To The Customer 134
   Alert The Customer About The Shipment 135
CHAPTER 7 - HOW TO FIND MANUFACTURERS AND SUPPLIERS 138
   Using Oberlo (Oberlo.Com) 138
   Run A Targeted Google Search 139
   Use Online Directories 140
   Go To Trade Shows 142
   Spy On Your Competitors 143
   Contact Manufacturer To Find Distributors 143
   Domestic Supplier Vs International Suppliers 144
   What To Look For In A Good Supplier 145
   Identifying Fake Wholesalers 146
CHAPTER 8 - HOW TO OPERATE YOUR BUSINESS 148

CHAPTER 9 - DEALING WITH PRODUCT RETURNS AND CUSTOMER SERVICE 157
   Ensure You Understand Your Supplier's Return Policy 157
   How To Create Your Own Product Return Policy 159
   How To Handle The Return Process 161
   In Summary, The Return Process Should Be As Follows: 164
CHAPTER 10 - HOW TO SCALE YOUR BUSINESS 166
   Run Adverts On Social Media 167
   Cultivate Customer Trust In Your Business 168
   Retarget Customers Who Visit Your Site Without Making A Purchase 169
   Use Social Media To Drive Traffic 170
   Start A Blog To Drive Organic Traffic To Your Dropshipping Store 171
   Use Pop-Ups To Get Your Visitors To Subscribe 171
   Find Online Forums Where Your Niche Is Discussed 172
   Use Market Analytics To Monitor Your Progress 173
BONUS 1 - HOW TO DROPSHIP WITH SHOPIFY 175
   Choose A Name For Your Dropshipping Store 176
   Create A New Shopify Account 176
   Set Up Your Account And Add All Necessary Information 177
   Launch Your Dropshipping Store 179
   Design And Personalize Your Store 179
   Add Products To Your Store 180
   Start Selling And Cashing In 182
BONUS 2 - HOW TO DROPSHIP ON AMAZON & EBAY 183
   Amazon 183
   Ebay 187
BONUS 3 - MISTAKES TO AVOID WHEN STARTING THE BUSINESS 190
   Starting Without Learning The Ins And Outs Of Dropshipping 190
   Choosing Bad Suppliers 191
   Lacking Faith In The Dropshipping Model 191
   Expecting Money To Come Easily 192
   Failing To Retarget Your Site Visitors 192
   Using Low-Quality Product Images 192
   Misleading Your Customers About Your Shipping Time 193
   Being Afraid To Reinvest Your Money In The Business 193
   Failing To Work With Instagram Influencers 194
   Using Complicated Shipping Fee Structures 194
   Creating Unclear Policies 195
   Mishandling Product Returns 195
   Relying Too Much On One Supplier 196
   Failing To Test Several Products 196
   Focusing On Price Competition 196
   Selling Products That Violate Trademark Or Copyright Laws 197
CONCLUSION 198

SHOPIFY

STEP BY STEP GUIDE ON HOW TO MAKE MONEY ONLINE

BRETT STANDARD

INTRODUCTION

First of all, I want to thank you for taking the time to choose and read my guide on making money with Shopify. This is a beginner's guide and it will walk you through what Shopify is, why you should use it, and how to set up your Shopify account. We will also be looking at some of the very best Shopify apps that you can use as well as delving into the technical side – adding pages, changing the way your Shopify website looks, and how to take payments, as well as all the Shopify plans on offer. Lastly, we look at how you can maximize your earning potential by using Shopify with Amazon and Facebook.

Shopify offers plenty of technical support and advice to help you along your way so even a true beginner can get started in just a short while. By the end of this guide, you will understand what Shopify is and how it can help you in your quest to earn money online.

Really and truthfully, it doesn't matter if you want to earn a bit of extra cash on the side or if you want to be the boss of your own empire, Shopify can help you. There is a kind of appealing side to running a business online, but it isn't without its challenges. It is going to be hard work to start with so don't think you can set this up in minutes and then sit back for an easy ride. You can do it though, provided you have the right ideas, you've done your homework and you are prepared to be in some blood, sweat and tears to do it.

Shopify is now the online store of choice for many entrepreneurs and has been the one method that has helped people to start the online business they always dreamed of starting. And, for those businesses already established, it is a great platform to help them diversify into e-commerce too.

In simple words, if you want a shop, whether you are selling small or are a huge going concern, you can have one with Shopify. And you can customize your store, upload as many products as you want and join the many thousands already making money with Shopify.

Once again, thank you for choosing my guide. Let's get started!

CHAPTER 1

WHAT IS SHOPIFY AND HOW DOES IT WORK?

No doubt you have already heard of Shopify. It is something of a household name now. Unless you have already delved deeply into it then the chances are you won't know what it can do for you and how it works so that's what I'm going to start by telling you before we look at the main advantages and disadvantages of using it.

So, what is it?

Shopify is a way of setting up a store online, providing you with an easy platform to sell just about anything that you want. It is incredibly popular with entrepreneurs and businesses who want an easy way to create an e-commerce shop that can operate alone or as part of an existing company.

SHOPIFY

One thing that sets Shopify aside from the competition is the fact that it is incredibly versatile. You don't need to have any experience in writing code. If all you want is a simple store to get up and running pretty much straight away, Shopify has a range of templates that you can choose from. These provide the skeleton of the store and can be customized so you can put your own unique stamp on your store. However, Shopify is not limited to small businesses or internet entrepreneurs; it is scalable, customizable and even multi-lingual, making it the perfect platform for any business even the biggest of brands like Red Bull, KKW Beauty, WaterAid and Budweiser – all using Shopify as their online store platform.

How does it Work?

Shopify is dead simple to use, one of the biggest reasons why it is so popular. It is a web-based software so there is no need to install it first. The platform is fully hosted by Shopify and this brings several advantages, including full customer support. There isn't any need to go through complex installations, worry about upgrades that might mess things up and you don't need to worry about any web servers – it's all done for you. And Shopify is compatible with all the major operating systems.

Setting up a store is simple, as you will see later. All you need to do is sign up for your free 14-day trial on Shopify and give it a go. Once the free trial period is up you need to decide whether to continue or not and which plan to choose. We'll be looking at those plans later on, but there are several to choose from, each with its own unique features and price. Then, you just need to decide on what to sell and add your payment details to pay for your subscription.

That's all there is to it. You can register a domain name so your Shopify store has the name you want it to have and if you already have a website or a domain name, simply integrate it all with Shopify - I'll show you how later.

Shopify Advantages

Shopify has several decent advantages and one of the biggest is that it offers more than 100 different themes for you to choose from for your storefront. This allows you to choose a professional look that also looks good on a mobile device. For those that have used WordPress, the approach to Shopify themes is quite similar – a store holds the themes and you can browse to choose what you want. Some are free, some require payment and you can also choose from themes set up for specific industries. These themes have been professionally designed and Shopify ensures that they consistent and compatible with its own software before they allow them into the store.

Another great advantage is the flexibility that Shopify offers, allowing to use the Shopify app store to add different functionalities. There are over 12oo apps to choose from and we'll be looking at some of them in a later chapter. Again, some of them are free while some are paid and you can pick and choose the ones that help make your store easier to use and to automate certain aspects of it. There are social media apps, customer service, inventory management, accounting, even shipping apps, all available to add to your store to help run your new business. All of this makes Shopify more than a simple store; it is a complete business solution, providing assistance for the backend as well as the frontend. And if you worried about installing the apps, don't be because Shopify will do the work for you.

SHOPIFY

If there is one thing designed to send people into a panic, it's a glitch that causes their website to go down with no warning and leaving them with no idea how to get it all back again. Shopify is robust but, to deal with any issues that arise and any problems you may have their next advantage is that they operate a 24/7 customer support service. They offer several different phone numbers for different areas, they have email support and online chat so your problems can be solved straight away. Time is money as any business owner knows and the minimum amount of fuss and maximum speed to get an issue resolved is crucial.

The Shopify software is in the cloud so you have a great deal more flexibility because any web browser can be used to run it. You can work wherever you want, whenever you want, as long as you have a connection to the internet.

Security is not an issue either; Shopify does it all for you, ensuring all transactions are completely secure so you can concentrate on selling your goods.

Lastly, there is a Shopify POS (point of sale) app for both Android and iOS that helps take care of in-person transactions. Using it means you can sell anywhere – at a market, a fair, in a popup window, anywhere you want. Plus it offers the versatility of accepting multiple methods of payment. The best of it is, the app fully syncs with your account so your orders can be monitored as can stock levels in real time, across all your points of sale – online, physical store, and so on.

Shopify Disadvantages

While Shopify has plenty of advantages, it also has a few disadvantages. Don't be too surprised; nothing is perfect and nothing can possibly suit everyone so make sure you are aware of the downsides before you start.

Unless you make use of the Shopify payments system, you will need to pay a fee on each sale and that can be anywhere from 0.5% to 2%, depending on which plan you are signed up to. If you opt for the basic plan, the transaction fee is 2% of each sale; the Shopify Plan is 1% and the Advanced Plan is 0.5%. How much of a disadvantage this proves to be is down to your perspective. In terms of money, it is equal to between $0.50 and $2 for every $100 sale – that isn't too bad and that money is used to pay for the payment management technology that Shopify uses. In simple terms, all you are doing is paying them to handle your transactions. Plus, Shopify doesn't hide their fees; they are completely upfront and you will always know what the charges are going to be.

Not all the apps are free to use. While they can offer huge amounts of functionality, some of them do have a monthly cost attached to them and this can soon bump up your monthly expenditure. Take MailChimp, for example, a popular mail app that helps you to run a mail campaign. If you have less than 2000 email subscribers then Mailchimp is free, but any more and the costs are anywhere between $10 and $200 per month. Another one, FreshBooks, is a great accounting app but it will set you back almost $32 a month.

As far as apps go, if you have a small business most of them are free. But, grow your business larger and you may have to start paying out for those apps. For someone like you who is going to be starting a brand-new business, for now, you won't need to worry about that. And, if your business does grow, your revenue should grow with it and those all-important apps won't seem quite so expensive. You could try doing the accounting and marketing yourself to start with, but you will find that your attention will be on that and not on selling. You could also hire an external person to do for you, but that will definitely cost you more than the app would. Perhaps, in the long run, the best option is to bit the bullet and buy the app, saving yourself the time that you could be using to focus on selling.

Many platforms make use of CSS or HTML coding, but Shopify doesn't. Instead, it uses something called Liquid so store customization means you need to know the language or you need to know someone who does. That can prove expensive so, to begin with, stick with the themes on offer and leave the customization for later down the line.

While Shopify is incredibly flexible, and it can be highly customized, some parts of it can't unless you opt for the very expensive Shopify Plus plan so be aware of that from the start.

So, as you can see, most of the disadvantages revolve around costs and expense but, if you want a successful business, those are inevitable – you can't have it all for nothing. If you had a physical store, for example, you would have overheads in rent and utilities, not to mention taxes, staff, inventory and so on. With Shopify, the monthly subscription you choose is akin to these costs but much cheaper.

Let's move on and look at the different plans Shopify offers.

CHAPTER 2

THE DIFFERENT SHOPIFY PLANS

Now you know what Shopify is and how it works, let's take a look at what plans are on offer. Which one you choose will be determined by how large your business is and what your requirements are. There are five plans to choose from:

- Basic Shopify
- Shopify
- Advanced Shopify
- Shopify Lite
- Shopify Plus

Before we look at each one in a little more detail, bear in mind that Shopify offers domains for $9 a month. There are also monthly and yearly options for payment and you can upgrade or downgrade whenever you want with no charge. The only difference will be the difference in the payments. If this is your first time with Shopify, you are better off starting with monthly payments. There are no cancellation charges when you are paying annually, but you also won't get a refund of any unused portion of the payment. Test things out first by paying monthly – you won't lose so much if things don't work out.

The Plans

When you land on the Shopify page detailing their plans you will only see the first three options from the list above. You will find the Lite and Plus plans detailed at the bottom of the page. Lite is the cheapest plan and Plus is the most expensive. A quick rundown of what you can expect to pay:

- Shopify Lite - $9/month
- Basic Shopify - $29/month
- Shopify - $79/month
- Advanced Shopify - $299/month
- Shopify Plus – prices start at about $2000 per month but are variable.

Each of the plans also has their own credit card rates and these are what you will get charged if you choose the Shopify Payments option to manage transactions and payment processes. Basically, when a purchase is made from your Shopify store, you get charged by the payment processor – the system that collects your money and places it onto your bank. Credit card rates are handling fees for transferring money from the purchases to the seller. These are normal and you cannot avoid paying them – at the end of the day, it means you don't need to meet every one of your customers in person, collect the cash and then deposit it into your own bank account.

Let's delve into the plans.

Shopify Lite

At $9 a month, Shopify Lite is the cheapest plan and it provides only the very basic features, such as:

- A Facebook selling channel
- Payment tools – for credit card and other forms of payment
- A couple of Buy buttons.

It is advertised separately to the main plans because, technically, it isn't really an online store. Instead, it provides access to a couple of features that can be added to an existing website, blog or social media account, enabling you to sell on a small scale. It also has a neat feature that allows you to connect Facebook Messenger on your Facebook business page to your account on Shopify. This lets you chat instantly with your customers and provide a very quick solution for customer support.

If you do not have a website or a blog already set up and doing well then Shopify Lite isn't for you. The idea behind Lite is so that it can be added to an existing online platform that already has its own domain and hosting in place. It's perfect if you have those platforms and just want to sell a few items – installing Shopify Lite to your website is really quite simple.

Shopify Basic

Shopify Basic costs $29 per month and this one will provide you with an online store with lots of useful features. These features include:

- An engine for discount codes
- Uploading as many items as you want to your store
- Tools for fraud analysis
- Unlimited storage for files
- 24/7 technical support
- SSL certificate for encryption and security
- Manual order creation

The plan also comes with a blog and a website, ensuring that everything is linked together as it should be and fully managed through Shopify. You get everything you need to create an online store that is fully functional and looks professional. The store can be used whether you have a website or blog or not.

The credit card rate is 2.9% plus $0.30 for each transaction on top of the monthly fee.

Shopify

This is the middle plan and is, so far, the most popular. It is, however, $79 per month, a fair bit more than the Basic plan. The reason it is so popular is that it offers pretty much every Shopify feature you could possibly need.

You get everything the Basic plan offers plus some extras, including:

- Professional reports

- Recovery for abandoned carts
- A gift card feature

The abandoned cart tool is quite useful because it stores all the information from those who visit, start adding to the shopping cart but don't finish off their order. By retaining their information, you can then contact the customer later – they were obviously interested enough to start shopping so you can try to encourage them to finish. However, instead of you needing to make contact with each of these customers individually, you also have the tools to automate the process by automatically sending a customized email to them. You can even decide when the email should be sent, from a matter of hours after they abandon the shopping cart to days.

Why is this such an important feature? Simply because research has shown that almost 70% of online customers abandon their cart before completing a purchase but, when they are contacted later, they often end up spending up to 50% more. This isn't just good for gaining sales, it also helps you to determine why the initial sales are not being completed. Perhaps your store is a bit confusing or the purchasing process takes too long and customers give up. These are all things you need to know so you can put them right and make things easier for customers.

If you are thinking about growing your business quickly then the features of this plan, such as unlimited storage and unlimited products are great. This plan is also ideal for those who already earn more than $5,000 a month through online sales – the transaction fee is cheaper than the Basic. Plus, the abandoned cart recovery feature is worth paying a bit more for because it could potentially increase your earnings quite significantly.

The credit card rate is 2.6% and $0.30 per transaction.

Advanced Shopify

Costing $299 a month, Advanced Shopify is not cheap, but it does offer quite a few advantages for the large businesses. As well as everything from the Basic Plan and the Shopify Plan, Advanced also offers pretty much unlimited everything:

- Unlimited product uploads
- Unlimited storage capacity
- Unlimited uploads for posts and videos
- Unlimited abandoned cart recovery package
- Shipping discounts
- Advanced reporting
- Adding access for up to 15 different users

The money saved on the shipping discounts and transaction fees make this the ideal plan for a business earning $10,000 or more every month. It also allows for shipping to be taken care of by another party and provides business reports that offer more detail so you can analyze data, test out different variables for marketing and try to make projections for the future.

The credit card rate is 2.4% plus $0.30 per transaction.

Shopify Plus

The final plan is Shopify Plus, the plan that proves this is more than just a platform for selling small amounts of simple goods. This is for the big companies and organizations and it provides management for all orders and operations for every sale. You also get 200 TB storage capacity, more than enough for even the largest store and the biggest benefit is no transaction fees.

However, you can't sign up for this plan through the website. Instead, you must call Shopify direct and discuss your requirements with them to get a quote. The minimum fee is $2,000 per month though.

This is a highly customizable option giving you the opportunity to adapt it to your branding and requirement; the level of technical and customer support is excellent, as it should be when you fork out that kind of cash every month, and you get a dedicated account manager working with you all the way.

The Shopify Plus platform can handle large visitor volumes easily, and there are no issues with processing potentially thousands of sales every minute, making this the ideal plan for the largest of businesses. It's ideal for the company that wants to concentrate on sales, customer service, and marketing, automating the rest as far as possible and leaving it to a third party to deal with.

How Do You Choose a Plan?

That is going to come down to a few factors, such as your monthly budget and the size of your company. If you run a blog and want to sell just a few products per month through your own website then the Lite plan will be sufficient.

If you have a store already but with another provider, Shopify helps you to make the transfer easily. The other way to determine which plan is right for you is to use the data you already have on sales, customers, stock, and so on.

CHAPTER 3

SHOPIFY FEATURES

We mentioned some of the features that are available on each of the plans so now we'll look at them in a little more detail.

Features for Every Plan:

Every Shopify Plan comes with these features:

- **Unlimited Products** – you can upload unlimited products to your store with no restrictions

- **Unlimited Bandwidth/Unlimited Storage** - this is important. You can have as many visitors as you like and upload as many videos and photos as you want without being charged any extra

- **Shopify POS** – this is the Point-of-Sale feature, a neat tool that lets you make sales at a physical store, be it a market, fair, or so on. The POS app must be installed to your Android or iOS device and you can then process sales and transactions anywhere you want, as well as managing your store from within your Shopify account

- **Channel for Online Sales** – with this, you can use several sales channels – your Shopify store, social media accounts, and so on. Everything is seamlessly integrated so you can manage everything in one place, monitoring orders, transactions and everything across all channels.

- **Fraud Analysis** – this is added in Shopify Payments automatically, helping you to track potentially fraudulent orders and alerting you to any risks. This ensures your transactions are legitimate and you avoid losses.

- **Discount Codes** – discount codes are a good way of enticing people into your store, building up a bigger audience and more potential sales. If you use Instagram, you may have spotted one or two influencers who provide fans with unique codes to use with specific brands. Well, these are the codes that the Shopify plans give you. How you give them to your audience is entirely up to you; you could ask influencers or bloggers to give your store a bit of promotion in exchange for something, you could give the codes out to first-time buyers to give them some kind of incentive or you could use them in a targeted email drive – it's up to you.

- **Overview** - each plan provides you with an overview of your key sales data. This will tell you your overall sales numbers, how many visitors your store gets, how many orders are placed and so on. You are also provided with finance reports showing your income, expenditure and any transactions that are pending.

- **Customer Service** – Shopify provides you with several ways to contact them and they are operational 24/7. With the Lite plan you get an email address and Live Chat, with all others you also get phone numbers to call them on.

- Those are the features on every plan; let's look at what the other features are:

The Basic Plan

- These features are not available on Lite but are available on the Shopify and the Advanced Plans:

- **Online Store** - this is a platform that is customizable to your requirements and used for displaying and selling your products. It is, in essence, the only way that your customers see your brand and the only place where you can track every order, transaction, all your products, stock levels and customer information for your store. It has a blog and website built into it so these can be run beside your store, ensuring your products are linked to great content that tells your audience what you are selling, to reach out to new customers and get some much-needed feedback.

- **SSL Certificate** - this tool ensures that you and your customers have a secure connection between the browser and the server. Your information is safe as are the details your customers provide. When activated, a small SSL padlock shows in the address bar, telling your customers they are visiting a secure site.

The Shopify Plan

As well as the features on the Basic plan, this plan also has a few extras that the basic plan doesn't have. These extras can make all the difference in the brand experience you give your customers:

- **Gift Cards** – discount codes are good, but gift cards go the extra step. Where a discount code is valid for one visit, gift cards can be used on multiple visits to your store. It is also a good way of getting new customers as your existing ones can buy them as gifts for friends and family who then go on to become a customer of yours. Shopify has different prices for gift cards so your customers get the flexibility of choice. As well as that, you get the ability to show off your branding by customizing the gift card.

- **Professional Reports** – these are helpful in letting you analyze the way your customers make purchases. They show sales by product, helping you to organize your store format better, to prepare for changes that are seasonal and pan your marketing and ad campaigns. You also see information about your customers and the way they interact with your Shopify store. For example, you will see how many first-time visitors you have had, return customers, customers by country, one-off or repeated purchases and more.

- **Abandoned Cart Recovery** – we talked about his in the last chapter. If your budget allows, it is definitely worth upgrading your plan to get this feature because it can potentially increase your sales quite significantly. This is an especially helpful feature for high-traffic stores.

The Advanced Shopify Plan

- In addition to the features on the Basic and Shopify plans, the Advanced Plan also offers these features:

- **Custom Report Builder** - with this, you can make reports that are customized and unique, allowing you a better understanding of what happens on your site. For example, if you have an ad campaign on the go to try to increase traffic, you can get a report that tracks that campaign by linking it to traffic and relevant sales. This is great for testing the performance of campaigns and using the data to create new strategies.

- **Calculated Carrier Shipping** – finally, you get a feature that allows for the integration of other shipping services into your store. This is beneficial in two ways – first, the shopping rates are exact when a customer makes a purchase and, second, you shoppers get a choice of delivery options, including one-day, express and standard.

Other Features

- While that covers the main features of each plan, there are a few others that may not be aware of in Shopify:

- **Customer Profiles** – customers can be asked to create an account before they can start shopping. With this, you can track all their transactions, works out your best customers and what they are buying. Why would you need to know this? So that your email and marketing campaigns can be customized, so you can set up loyalty rewards for the best customers, and you can use their purchase history to send them emails. For example, let's say a customer purchased a special daytime moisturizing cream from you. You could email them when you estimate that they will be running out of it, giving them the chance to make another purchase.

- **Shopify With Facebook** - This is a great feature for those who have large Facebook followings. When you integrate Shopify with Facebook, your customers can make their purchase directly from your Facebook page without needing to open your site. This is easier and convenient for the customers and these are deciding factors in making or breaking sales. Facebook will also sync to Shopify, ensuring your transactions are updated on both platforms.

- **Drop-Shipping** – you can also use your Shopify store to do drop-shipping. This way, you can sell the products without having to purchase them first. A customer will make a purchase from your store; the order is sent to a third-party supplier; they send the product out to the customer. The customer won't know where the product is coming from and you get to save money on inventory costs.

- **Future Publishing** – to help with time management, future publishing allows you to line up content for publishing on set days and times in the future. The content won't show until that specified date and time. You can spend time writing weeks or months' worth of work, which can be published when you want it to, saving time later down the line.

- **Two-Step Authentication** – your store will be secure from hackers who might be able to steal passwords and other sensitive data. Even if a hacker did manage to get your password, the two-factor authentication would make it hard for them to get into your about as they would not be able to verify the login through the code sent to your mobile phone, And, if you get a code out of the blue, you'll know that a hacker is lurking.

CHAPTER 4

WHY USE SHOPIFY?

So, who benefits from using Shopify? Anyone who wants to run a business with a minimum amount of hassle, for a start. If you went to a hotel and the hot water wasn't working, you would call the front desk and report it; they would have to fix it. If you are the hotel owner, it's down to you to fix things; running a Shopify store is running the hotel!

Let's say that you have kids and, while they are at school, you need something to do with your time. A Shopify store will give you that something as well as potentially earning you the money to contribute to the household. In the same way, college students could earn some extra income.

If you already have a product but don't know how to go about selling it, Shopify is ideal. It provides you the all-inclusive e-commerce platform you need to get your products up for sale online.

And lastly, if you already have a fulltime job but really want to be your own boss, Shopify is a great starting point. Obviously, you shouldn't ditch your job straightaway but using Shopify will give you an idea of whether you can make enough money to go it alone.

Why You Should Choose Shopify:

- It's not expensive and because it's so easy to use you get to focus on selling without having to worry about maintaining a website

- There are tons of designs and layouts for your store, all provided by Shopify, and many of them are completely free. If you want a new look every couple of months you can have one. If you need something more specialized, the Shopify design pros will do it for you – at a cost of course.

- Any changes to your site can be made discoverable by all the big search engines. You have an unmatched ability to put in whatever information you want, such as titles, descriptions, and so on. This helps you to make your store SEO-friendly.

- If you need help, it's there, 24/7. Things happen that are outside of our control and a bit of technical help is needed to get things back up and running quickly, providing you with complete peace of mind.

- Internet security is a huge concern with online shoppers these days and we hear far too many stories about identity theft and credit card fraud. Both you and your shop customers can be reassured that Shopify spends a lot of money on security, using SSL and HTTPS to keep their site secure.

- You can spend as little as $29 a month to run a Shopify store. Shopify keep their prices affordable so that pretty much anyone can have their own store.

- Shopify gives you everything you need to get off and running very quickly, just minutes in some cases. You need little in the way of technical experience or skills and complete beginners can use Shopify with ease. Start small and grow or choose your plan and stay put, it's up to you.

- Shopify offers more than online stores. You can also join in if you run a physical store using the Shopify POS app, a complete package that requires no third party to be involved.

Before we start looking at how to set up your Shopify online store, we'll take a quick look at some of the best apps that Shopify offers to help you with your business.

CHAPTER 5

TOP SHOPIFY APPS

Shopify is, without a doubt, a great e-commerce platform. It is affordable, it is easy to use and you can get set up and running right out of the box in a very short time. It isn't just a storefront; you get checkouts that are fully featured so retailers can begin taking payments from their customers straight away and Shopify Shipping makes fulfilling orders a breeze, managing the entire process for you. And Shopify also has the tools to deal with marketing for you – you can have automated emails sent and Shopify can even come up with targeted social marketing campaigns.

Basically, Shopify makes starting an e-commerce business and growing it very simple. If you want an online store or you want to move an already-existing online store to a more user-friendly platform, then Shopify is a great choice. However, while it offers all you need to get your store off the ground, you can make things a good deal better by using some of the add-ons that Shopify offers in the form of apps. We're going to look at some of the best apps you can use with your Shopify store:

- **Edit Order**

Edit Order is designed to help you edit completed orders, which means altering orders that were placed incorrectly (wrong size, wrong color, etc.). You can also change billing addresses, and order prices, as well as streamlining your policy for returns. The app is $14.99 per month with a 14-day free trial.

- **Audience Push**

This is a vital app for any Shopify store owner who also uses Facebook for advertising. Once your Facebook account is connected to Shopify (a single-click achieves that) Audience Push updates the Facebook Custom Audience List automatically with all new customer information. This can save you a huge amount of time. The app is $9 per month with a 14-day free trial.

- **Order Printer**

The ability to print receipts, orders and packaging labels is a vital part of any e-commerce store, but this is not a standard part of Shopify. That means Order Printer is a crucial app. The document design and layout is completely customizable and you can also print in bulk to save some time. This is a free app.

- **Persistent Cart**

Persistent Cart is one of the easiest apps to install and can save sales for you. If a customer leaves your site without going through checkout, the app will save their cart. That cart will then be available, exactly as it was, when they come back, even if they are using a different device. There is a free version of the app, but it doesn't offer anywhere near the features of the paid app which costs just $3.99 per month with a 30-day free trial.

- **Google Shopping**

Google Shopping is one of the in-house apps that help you to up your sales without too much effort. It works by automating the way you list products on Google Shopping or the way they are listed as Product Listing Ads. Once you connect it, the app syncs your store automatically with the Google Merchant Center, allowing listings to be updated from right within Shopify. The app is free to install, but there may be additional charges.

- **Tidio Live Chat**

Most customers want instant communication with a company and demand a Live Chat feature on a website. This is because they can get an answer to their question straightaway, improving efficiency and better levels of customer satisfaction. Tidio enables integration of Live Chat though their plugin and the app is free although additional charges may apply.

- **Exit Offers**

The Exit Offers app can help to increase your sales by saving customers that are about to leave your site without making a purchase. When they add products to the shopping cart and then go to leave without finishing, you can show them an offer that is designed to make them want to buy. That offer is down to you, but it could be a certain percentage off their order, free shipping, or something like it. The app costs $9.99 per month with a 14-day free trial.

- **Orderify**

Orderify gives your customers better control over what they purchase. They can edit their orders, cancel them (provided they haven't been shipped) and even reorder previous purchases very easily, leading to happy customers and more sales. The app costs $4.99 per month with a 30-day free trial.

- **McAfee SECURE**

Most customers prefer to make their purchases from a store they can trust and if they feel at all uncomfortable about adding their card details to your site, they won't do it. McAfee SECURE is a widget that provides that element of trust, showing your customers that they can trust your site 100%. The app is free, but additional charges may apply.

- **Oberlo**

Oberlo is a great little app for helping you to find a product for selling or a business idea. Using Oberlo, search a marketplace containing products that can be directly imported to your Shopify store. When an order comes in, Oberlo ships straight to your customers, eliminating the need for you to worry about packaging the goods and shipping them. This is a free app, but additional charges may apply.

- **Klaviyo**

Klaviyo provides you with a very powerful package for email marketing automation at business-level speeds. One click integrates Klaviyo with your Shopify store and you can easily set up autoresponders, such as an email about abandoned carts, welcome emails, follow-ups on order and so on. The app is free to download.

- **Product Reviews**

With Shopify Product Reviews, you can add a feature to your products for customers to leave reviews. This way, your customers get another way of engaging with you and with each other, a great way of encouraging sales. This is a free app.

- **Plug in SEO**

Plug In SEO is an app that shows you at a glance if there are any SEO issues with your site that need to be fixed. The app will check the homepage of your store and display its verdict, providing details of where fixes need to be made. The app has a free plan available and 7-day completely free trial.

- **Facebook Store**

With Facebook Store you can show off your products on your Facebook page and sell them too. Your customers can share products with their follower, friends and family and you get a much wider reach in terms of audience and traffic. The app is free to install.

- **Bulk Discounts**

With Bulk Discounts you can import discount codes directly to your store or you can create them to dish out to your customers. This is a free app.

- **Free Shipping Bar**

Free Shipping Bar provides you with a slide bar that you can use for showing offers for free shipping. It can also show messages as customers add items to their carts and congratulate your customers on getting the free shipping offer. This is free to install, but there are other similar apps that may offer more and charge a small monthly fee.

- **ALT Text**

ALT Tet generates the ALT text for the images in your store automatically. This will be based on a specified parameter set and is designed to drive more traffic your way from the search engines. The app costs $1.99 per month.

- **Yotpo**

Yotpo is a useful app that helps you to easily generate reviews for your products. These can then be shared across your social media profiles to help drive more traffic and more potential sales. It is free to install, but there are priced plans available for premium business customers.

- **Printful**

With the Printful app, you can sync with your store for drop shipping custom products like printed t-shirts, mugs, etc. The order come via your store and goes to Printful to print and ship for you. This is a free app.

- **Improved Contact Form**

With Improved Contact Form you can create a contact form that pops up in your store, telling you the location of the customer and which pages they looked at before they made contact with you. It is a free app, but additional charges may apply.

- **Better Coupon Box**

Better Coupon Box is designed to help you covert all visitors to your store into potential customers. When a customer goes into your store for the first time, they will see a gorgeous popup that offers them a specific discount if they follow you on your Twitter, Facebook, or other social media profiles. This is a free app.

- **AfterShip**

With AfterShip, you can keep track of every shipment in one central place and let your customers have regular delivery updates. Support is provided for more than 350 carriers including UPS, DHL, FedEx, USPS, and more. There is a free plan although more features are offered with paid plans and there is a 14-day free trial.

- **eBay Professional Importer**

This app takes the catalog from your eBay store and copies it over to your Shopify store. All products are supported, including active, unsold and scheduled and will also handle all the images, categories, and variations automatically. The app starts at $14.95 per month and there is a 30-day free trial.

- **Shippo**

Shippo allows you to integrate all orders on your Shopify store and print shipping labels with a single click. You can choose the dimensions of your parcels, data for pickup, type of service, your preferred carrier, and so on and your labels are provided within seconds. The app is free to install, but there may be additional charges.

- **Social Media Stream**

Social Media Stream lets you showcase your Twitter, Facebook, Instagram, Pinterest, YouTube and Tumblr posts on one page, helping you to get more followers on your social media accounts and cut down the time you have to spend embedding posts and images. There is a free plan available, but additional charges may apply.

- **Digital Downloads**

Digital Downloads gives you the opportunity to include digital products in your store. Customers can have instant access to the content and any updates to the products are sent to the customers automatically. This is a free app.

There are thousands more apps to choose from, but these will give you a good head start in making the most of your Shopify store. Although your budget may dictate that you only go for the free apps, do bear in mind that the paid versions of apps tend to offer more features and, to be fair, provided you do your marketing, the money you pay out can be recouped pretty quickly.

CHAPTER 6

SETTING UP YOUR SHOPIFY STORE

Setting your store up is actually quite easy once you know which features you want to use so that's what we are going to do now — set up the store, add a product and come up with a URL that will allow your customers to recognize you online.

Choose Your Platform

First, you must work out which service and platform you want to use. Let's see what the services are first. Well, this applies to the pricing plans we looked at in an earlier chapter. Most of these are pretty much identical in features, but the more expensive plans have more advanced features. And don't forget that credit card fee per transaction on top of the monthly fee for the service.

For those just getting their foot in the door, the lowest service is probably the best as it gives you a chance to test the waters and learn how things work before you upgrade. Once you get a handle on the basics and the money starts rolling in, you can choose to upgrade. Keep in mind that the Basic Shopify plan does come with quite a bit though.

Your next decision is which platform you want to use and by this, I am talking about the website you want your Shopify Store to be connected to. You can, if you choose, connect your store to several platforms at once so let's see which ones are available:

Facebook:

Facebook has a built-in store option and when Shopify is connected, your page will allow customers to either visit your store or purchase from right there on your Facebook page. If you have a page that is often shared, this can be a great idea because you get access to a wider audience who can see your products instantly and decide whether they want to buy straight away and see what else you have for sale. This works for those who have a large following on the social media platform.

Pinterest Buttons:

Pinterest is still one of the biggest social media sites and quite easily outpaces Twitter in user participation and growth so it should not be pushed to the wayside. Shopify partners with Pinterest so you can link product pins to your Shopify account, allowing customers to buy instantly. Even better, the purchase takes place in the Pinterest app so your customers don't have to jump through a ton of hoops to get access to your products – this can increase your sales percentage quite significantly.

Shopify Store:

Shopify provides space in their store for you to set up an online shop. They have a drag-and-drop interface that helps you to create a great-looking storefront. The upside to this system is that is easy and eliminates the need to spend hours working on designing and building a website. Shopify provides strong support for their sales platform and they also offer app support for WordPress and other websites. Shopify has all the customization you want to get a great store up and running in just minutes.

Your Own Website:

WordPress and Squarespace are good options for websites, but they don't really work too well with Shopify. Shopify has put a lot of hard work in to come up with their own platform and, while you could use WordPress, it takes a lot of work and a knowledge of coding to integrate Shopify. You also won't be able to use the apps n the Shopify stores. We'll be starting by using the Shopify platform as it is much easier so let's get started.

1. Go to http://www.shopify.com and sign up for your free trial account. Input your email address and then click on Get Started.

2. Create a password and note it down so you can remember it.

3. Input your store name. If you don't really have one yet just type in anything; you can change it again later.

4. Click on Create Your Store

5. Next, you need to decide if it's an online store you want or you want to sell in a pop-up store or a physical store. For now, choose an online store because that will provide you with a website to sell your goods from.

6. Click on Next and then input your name and address. These details are used for setting up your Shopify account so they won't show up in your store. Your store details will be set up later.

7. Click the button for "This Is My Retail Store Address" ONLY if you want to use the name and address you input as your store address; if not, leave the box unticked.

8. Click on "Take Me To My Store." Nobody can see your store yet because it has been protected by a password and only those with the password can see it. You only remove that password when you are ready for your store to go live.

9. Now your store admin area is created. At the top of the browser window you will see a URL. Bookmark the page or write the URL down. This is your admin area, where your entire store is controlled. Click on "View Your Website" at the top of the screen and you will see your store.

That's it and your store is created and you are ready to start adding products.

CHAPTER 7

ADDING YOUR PRODUCTS

Right now, your store is looking a little bit empty so let's add a product and see what it looks like.

1. Click on "Back to Dashboard" so you go back to the Admin area and then click on "Add Products."

2. Pick a product that you have an image for already and type a descriptive title in into the text box for Title

3. Under the description, a number of fields will appear; fill them in with the correct details – these can be changed later so input anything for now.

4. Obviously, "Price" is what the product will be sold at and "Compare At Price" shows you what you sold the product for previously – this can be left blank if it doesn't apply to you.

5. Either input an SKU – a stock keeping unit – or leave it empty so one can be assigned. If you have an ISBN, an ASIN, or a barcode, the details go in the Barcode field. This lets the search engines easily index products, adding them, in Google's case, to their price comparison feature.

6. Lastly, decide if you are keeping an inventory and whether the "Out of Stock" option should be shown by Shopify so you don't sell any more than currently in stock. You can leave the box for "Multiple Options" blank for now.

7. Now click "Choose Files" and add some images of the product.

8. For the "Visibility" option choose visible so you can see your store with your newly added products. Once you have seen it, you can delete the product or make it invisible but, once again, because your website is password protected, nobody can see it or buy the product.

9. Click on "Save Product" and choose to "View in Website" – button at the top of the page.

Doesn't that look good? Add a few more products and then we'll move on to setting up your domain and emails.

CHAPTER 8

DOMAINS AND EMAILS

Before your store goes live there are a few other details you need to deal with and the first is your domain name. When you choose one of the three main plans you get given a domain name but it isn't very exciting and it will do nothing for your credibility online. All that domain name consists of is your name followed by .shopify.com. You need a domain that is going to scream your brand or your product from the rooftops and Shopify helps you to do this by letting you buy a domain name through a domain registrar. When you purchase through an external registrar, that name is yours for as long as you choose, even if you, one day, decide to move on from Shopify.

Use a reputable domain registrar, like GoDaddy. You will find that most offer much the same service but do your homework thoroughly and don't forget to read the small print!

Once you have chosen your domain registrar, type in the domain name you want and click on Search. You will see a list of the domain names that match or come somewhere near what you typed in. If the name has already been taken, you will need to think of another – tip: before you go looking for a registrar, spend some time thinking of several names that will suit your business. It's highly unlikely that you will get the one you really want!

Your name needs to be memorable, not too long and easy to spell. People don't like complicated website names and will tend to move on to an easier one! You should pay no more than about $15 a year for a domain name if it is not a premium com or co.uk name – these will set you back a little more.

Chose which name you want and click on the "Checkout button" and decide how long a term you want to pay for. Longer periods tend to work out cheaper per year and 2 years seems to be the best bet – it's long enough to give your business chance to shine but doesn't tie you in for too long.

Input your payment and address details but be aware; if people search Whois for your domain name this address will show up. If you don't want your address made public, you can pay for an extra privacy feature on most registrars.

Once you have successfully ordered and paid for your domain name, you get a confirmation email. Click on the link in the email and you will be redirected to your control panel. Now you are ready to add that name to your Shopify site.

Return to the Shopify dashboard and click the option for the "Domains" menu. Click "Add an Existing Domain." Type your new domain name in and click "Add Domain." On your screen you will see a DNS address – write this down, you will need it in a minute. Also, write down the URL from the address bar – yourdomainname.myshopify.com.

In the control panel for your domain name (whichever registrar you chose), click on the option for "Manage Domains." Choose your domain name from the dropdown list and then go to the top of the page. Click on DNS and scroll through the list, clicking on "Show Advanced DNS Options."

Click to "Add a New Record" and type in the DNS number you wrote down – it must be exact, something along the lines of 205.95.223.56 (not this number!). In the Host box, type in your domain name, omitting the www from it. TTL needs to be set to 300.

Repeat these steps with CNAME and input your domain information.

It will take a while for all this to start working but, when they do, you will be able to use your own domain name to access your Shopify store.

Back in the dashboard for your Shopify store, click on "Domains" and then on "Set as Primary." Click on "Save" and you are ready to move on to the next step.

Setting up your Email Account

Now that your domain is all set up it's time to look at emails. You need a minimum of one email account for the domain name and this can be used for all your Shopify store contact details. Later on, you can set up one for each department or person in your business if you want. When you purchase your domain name, the registrar will likely provide you with one email address and a number of forwarders so what you could do is set up a primary email account and use other addresses to forward emails to that main account. If you need extra mailboxes, you can buy upgrades.

In your domain registrar control panel, click on "Email" and then on "Add New Address." Where it says Account Name, type in what you want the email address to be, sticking with a generic name for now like sales or mail. This becomes your primary address.

Next, click on "Add New Forwarder" and input the addresses you require, forwarding them to the primary email address you created first.

Once your email account has been set up, you can use any email client to access them, but the easiest way is to use the client supplied by your domain account. So, find your main email account and click "Login" beside it. Input your email and your password and then click on "Compose."

Input a message, with a subject line and an email address to send it to – use your own personal one for this test – and click on "Send." Check your personal email account to make sure the email came through. Reply to it and then go back to your domain email account to make sure the reply came through okay. If it did, all is working well.

Now we can move on to setting up the remainder of your Shopify store.

CHAPTER 9

PAGES, DESIGN AND PAYMENTS

To set up the rest of your store, we need to create the pages you need, change the design of the site to suit you and add in how you will accept payments.

Creating Pages

We have a product or two in the store, we have our domain name and we have our email addresses. Now we want to make the store look like a proper store so we'll add some pages.

In your Shopify admin area click the "General" tab and go to the bottom of the page – a password is there, copy it and go back to your store webpage (the one with your domain name). Input that password.

Your store will look as it will to any visitor to it so look around, get the feel for it, click on stuff and make sure it all works. Once you have done that, you will have a better understanding of why you are going to be making the following changes.

We'll start with your front page; click on the prompt and you will go to your admin panel to the Pages section. Click on a page name and make some changes.

Input text as you would with any typing program. Give the customer a little information about you in your About Us page and also write what text is going to show up on the front page. Here, you can add other pages like a Contact Us page too.

Above the text window is a button for adding images; first, put your cursor in the position in the text you want the first image to appear and then click this button. Find your image (you should already have some saved on your computer for this). When you see the image in the window, click it and then click the box for "Size to Insert," choose the image size you want and then click the image icon again.

You will see that your image is in the text area, but none of the text wraps around it. If you want your image to show in between two paragraphs of text then you can leave this as it is but if you want the image within the text, we need to change it so click the image again and then click the Image icon.

Input a description for your image and then click the option to "Wrap Text Around Image." Add a little bit of spacing around your image – this will show as the white space between the text and the image.

Click on the button to "Edit Image," and you will see the text wrapped around your image with a nice white space separating it.

Go to the bottom of the area for text entry on the page and you will see some more fields to fill in – these are to do with the search engines, which will list websites that relate to the text content searched for by search engine users. Provide a description and a title – this is what is going to be seen in the search results when people look for you so make sure it is specific to the products or service you offer. You can leave the URL as is or provide a new one that uses good keywords. Lastly, click on "Save" and then on "Your Website>View" so you can see how your page looks.

Have a play around with the features on here and try adding other pages to the site. Once you are happy with what you have and are comfortable with creating pages, we'll move on to site design.

Changing Site Design

Your Shopify store is starting to take real shape now, but it still looks a bit, well plain and boring. Shopify provides you with the tools to create a stunning looking website with little effort and much of that is in the form of themes.

Go to your Shopify admin area and click on the "Themes" menu. Then click "Visit the Themes Store." On the left side of the store, choose "Free" and then choose any of the images to see information about a specific theme.

When you choose your theme, try to look beyond what you see in the product description; try to imagine your own store with the theme. Click the "View Demo" button to see the theme in action.

If you like it, you can see what it looks like on your own Shopify site. Close down the demo so you go back to the theme store. Click "Get Theme" and then click on "Publish As My Shop Theme."

Next, click on "Go To My Theme Manager" and you can edit certain parts of the theme, like the colors and you can also images if the theme includes a header image or an image slider. Click "Customize Theme" and you will be directed to the Theme settings. As you make changes, click "Preview" to see them – this way you can decide as you go if your changes work or not.

You can add a logo and an icon if you have them on your computer. You can change colors, fonts and so on and you will find that every change is self-explanatory. You can change it back very easily if you find it doesn't work or you can even just go ahead and get a different theme.

When you are finished, click on "Save Changes." Don't be afraid to experiment and try several free themes. This will give you an idea of what works and what doesn't for your specific shop. If you feel like splashing out, you can also choose a paid theme. These can be filtered by industry and feature so you can find what you want quite easily. Do take care over choosing your theme though; it has to work and it has to do exactly what you want it to do. The alternative is hiring a web designer to create a custom website and that is not cheap.

Taking Payments

So, you have a fantastic store, filled to bursting with fantastic products and a stream of traffic just waiting to visit. All a waste of time unless you have a way to take their money and this is where we use Payment Providers. When the Internet first took off, the banks were too slow to come forward and offer good methods for online payments to businesses so, naturally, a number of other companies stepped up to the plate and filled the gap. These payment providers are what link the shopping cart to your bank. Check the Shopify website for more details about payment providers that work together with Shopify.

PayPal

PayPal is, without a doubt, one of the most tried and tested methods for taking payments, not to mention one of the securest and easiest. To use PayPal with your Shopify account you need to set up a PayPal Merchant Account. Shopify automates this so it isn't even necessary for you to have a PayPal account already set up. Shopify will let you know by email when a product has been paid for and to prompt you into setting your account up. If you do have an existing PayPal account, just click on "Edit" and input your PayPal email address.

Credit Card Payments

Not everyone uses or wants to use PayPal, indeed some countries restrict usage or don't support it at all. However, there are other options and one of those is credit card payments – for some customers, this is much easier and it can be more cost effective for you as well. If you want to avoid a scenario where a customer abandons their cart before they pay for it, it is well worth considering using more respected providers, such as Nochex. If you are in the UK.

In terms of fees, here's how the Nochex and PayPal fees differ:

- **PayPal** – 3.4% plus £0.02 per transaction. On a £10 sale, you would pay £0.54 to PayPal, while £100 sales would cost you £3.60 in fees

- **Nochex** – 2.9% plus £0.20 per transaction. A £10 sale would cost £0.49 while a £100 sale would cost £3.10.

Small savings but, in the long run, it adds up to a whole lot of savings.

To set up credit card payments, from your admin control panel, click on "Accept Credit Cards" and click on "Select Credit Card Gateway." Register your chosen service and use the same email address that you registered the service within the box provided.

Click on "Activate" and the service will begin working in your store.

It makes sense to offer a range of payment options to cater to all customers. Not everyone will want to add a credit card and not everyone will want to use PayPal either. Explore the options open to you in Shopify and choose the options that work for you.

CHAPTER 10

BEFORE YOU GO LIVE

Before your store can go live, there are a few more things you need to do, especially if your store is selling physical and not digital goods. Shipping rates need to be set, including postage and packaging and you need to let Shopify know how tax needs to be dealt with. You will also need to give your customers a way of contacting you in the case of returns or problems.

Shipping Rates and Order Fulfillment

To set your shipping rates, from your control panel, click on "Shipping." Input whatever locations and rates that you want but the easiest is to have two – a home country rate and then a "Rest of the World" rate.

Further down the page, there are options for adding Drop Shipping or Order Fulfillment. These are not Shopify services and are run by third parties – some of them very recognizable names. This is a great way of selling products across the whole world without needing to send packages yourself. You send the drop shipping company a load of your products and they do everything for you – storage of stock, packaging and posting. And, because Shopify will integrate easily with these services, your sales can be handled by the other company without you getting involved in the order.

Tax Rates

If you earn over a certain threshold in most countries, there are tax or VAT systems in place. If tax has to be added to orders, click on "Tax" in the main admin panel and input the correct tax amount in the box for "Country Tax Rate." This will then appear on invoices and you will be able to see the tax you collected in your sales reports. If you don't have to collect any tax, this value can just be set as zero.

To see tax reports, click on "Reports" and then on "Tax Rate."

Contact Details

If you don't provide your customers with a way of contacting you, they are not likely to buy from you. So, in the main menu, tap on "Settings" and input your store details. All relevant email addresses must be included. Click on "Save" when you have finished.

Refund, TOS and Privacy Statements

In your main menu, click on "Settings" and then click on "Checkout" at the bottom of the page, you can set policy statements for refunds, privacy and terms of service. To do this, just click on the button for "Generate Sample" and then use the generated statements or change them to suit your requirements.

Important note – make sure you do this ONLY after contact details have been input to ensure that the correct details go into the statements.

Payment Plans

Earlier we looked at the payment plans, now you need to choose one. By now you have had time to look at Shopify and see how it works and whether it will suit your business. If it does, go ahead and choose the plan you want.

Your store is now ready to go live. Check it over one more time to make sure and then remove that password – your store is now out in the wild and open for business.

CHAPTER 11

DO'S AND DON'TS

When you first start to use Shopify, there are a few things that you should be aware of, things to do and things that you should NOT do:

- DO make sure that your audience is properly targeted. If you do this, it's a pretty safe bet that your efforts will be reaching potential visitors that may convert to sales.

- DON'T design your shop website to be difficult for people to navigate. Not all of your audience will be tech-savvy and you can bet that they don't want to jump through hoops to get what they want. Keep it simple, not highly technical.

- DO add new content on a regular basis. Not only do customers like to see new products, so do the search engines. When your customers see the same old products every time they visit, they are liable to start looking elsewhere for their goods.

- DO use backlinks on your website where you can. How? Find an expert or authority on your specific niche and approach them about writing a guest post for them. You can add a couple of links without it looking like blatant advertising.

- DO learn about SEO or search engine optimization. Getting this right makes you far more visible in a good way on the internet.

- DO use the right keywords. They must fit naturally with your products and they must be appealing, drawing in users and making the search engines your friend.

- DO make each page on your website appealing to users. Customers can lad on any one of your pages and they want to see something great.

- DO think about using internal links to go to the different pages you have but do NOT make all your pages look like each other. Even more important, the homepage must be completely different from all the other pages.

- DO make your homepage look eye-catching with images – perhaps of your product being used by people. Also, use colors and link to the other pages on your websites.

- If your store also has a blog DO keep things simple. Your theme will likely have its own blog format so stick to using that. Your customers want to see great content otherwise they won't come back.

- DO try to use long tail search terms. These are the terms that users are likely to input into a search engine. For example, instead of searching for "winter boots," a person is likely to be more specific, perhaps "knee-length winter boots" or "winter boots with fur trim." By being more specific, a user is more likely to find what they want.

- DO use your blog. If you start it, finish it. Visitors don't like blogs that only have new content added on rare occasions. They want to see regular, high quality, unique and relevant content. They want you to entice them to buy and your blog posts should always ask the customer to make a purchase. If you can't commit to updating this regularly then don't start it in the first place.

As a final check before you do go live, run through this list and make sure that you can tick every one of them off as complete:

1. Have you chosen the plan that suits you the best?
2. Have you chosen and purchased a punchy domain name?
3. Have you chosen the right theme for your store?
4. Have you uploaded enough products?
5. Have you added your social media accounts?
6. Have you picked out the Shopify apps that will benefit you the most?

7. Is your store set up so it can take payments from customers?
8. Have you got all the hardware you require?
9. Have you worked out a marketing plan centered on social media?

If you have done everything and you are happy with the way your store looks, you are ready to go live.

BONUS CHAPTER

SHOPIFY AND AMAZON

Have you considered the benefits of integrating your Shopify store with Amazon? Let's face it, you really can't go too far wrong by using the largest online marketplace in the world and taking your brand to the next level. Shopify stores are great for showing off your brand and for offering a high level of control over the experiences your customers have. But for the right kind of business, using Amazon as a marketplace too can boost your sales by opening your store to a whole new audience.

The Benefits

The benefits of integrating Shopify and Amazon are numerous:

- You can create your listings on Amazon in multiple categories directly from Shopify
- If your products are on Amazon, you can create offers in any category directly from Shopify

- Your product details can be synced, as can images and variants, to your Seller Central account on Amazon

- Shopify products can be linked to existing listings on Amazon

- You can set prices and reserve a specific amount of inventory just for Amazon

- Shopify reports can be used to reconcile your Amazon revenue

- Shopify syncs tracked inventory data with Amazon

- Amazon orders can be fulfilled from Shopify

Using Shopify To Sell on Amazon

Following these steps, you can easily use Shopify to sell your products on Amazon:

First, you need to make sure that your Shopify store meets all the requirements:

- You must have a Shopify account signed up to any of the plans and it must be active

- The products you sell must fit into a category that is supported

- You must be able to list process in either CAD or USD

- You must not be making use of Fulfillment by Amazon to ship your goods

You can add any listings you already have on Amazon to your Shopify account even if they do not fall into a supported category.

The next step, if you don't have one already, is to create a Professional Seller account with Amazon and you can do this by going to Seller Central. You must also ensure that, regardless of which Amazon store you use, you can also sell on Amazon.com

It is free to add the sales channel, but your Professional Seller account will cost you $39.99 per month, plus referral fees, which are based on the category your product falls into. To get set up with an account:

- Go to Amazon Services and click the button that says, "Start Selling."

- Complete the details required – name, password, email address

- When the account has been created there are five steps to finish the setup. You will need to have certain information available:

    o Name, address and telephone number of your business

    o Credit card details for the monthly fee

    o Bank account details for sales revenue

    o TIN no (Tax ID No – US only)

SHOPIFY

- Once your account has been created, you need to make sure your product categories need to be approved by Amazon. If they do, you need to apply for it.

- Next, your Shopify store can be given the Sales Channel:

    o In Shopify, go to "Sales Channels" and click the + button next to it

    o Go to the "Amazon by Shopify" option and click on "Learn More"

    o Click on "Add Channel" and then on "Connect to Amazon."

    o Follow the on-screen prompts to get your Shopify and Amazon accounts integrated; when finished you will automatically go back to Shopify

- Most of the categories will require a product identifier so that sellers can create new pages for their products and list them on Amazon. A UPC is the most common, but if you don't provide one, or an ISBN or EAN, you will see an error message. At this point you will need to add in the required details to go any further. If your products are being resold (i.e., through affiliate marketing) you might find they already have that identifier and you can use that. If you do need to purchase one, the official UPC supplier is GS1, but there are other resellers that may do them a little cheaper.

- If this is your first time selling anything on Amazon, and your products are in the supported categories, you can go ahead and do your Amazon listing from in Shopify:
    - Go to "Amazon" and click it to find the sales channel you installed
    - Click on "Create Listing"
    - Look in your Shopify catalog to find the product you want and click on "Select Product."
    - If your product is your own brand, complete the details required in the box
    - If you are reselling and this is not your brand, click on "Search" and see if that same product has already been listed. If you see one in the list that matches your product, click on "Select" and create your Offer.
    - Complete all the required detail for whichever option you choose and then click on "Publish."
- If you have products on Amazon already, regardless of category, you can claim them in your Shopify store. Also, if you want to add products in categories not supported by Shopify, you can add them to Amazon and then you can add them to your store.

Any listing that has been associated with your Amazon Professional account can be seen in your Shopify store under Amazon listings.

- Click "Link Products" and find the listing you want to be linked.

- Click "Browse Products" and look for the specific product, making sure you add the variants to your listing too.

- Now we need the tracking policy for the inventory. Every Amazon listing in your Shopify store needs one and you can choose between the store settings or manual management. If you opt for manual inventory management, you can reserve a portion of your stock purely for Amazon customers and, obviously, as each purchase is made, the inventory will drop and you will need to manually add more to it. Choosing the Shopify store settings, each product has a choice of three scenarios:

  - Shopify will track your inventory

  - Shopify will not track your inventory

  - Customers may purchase products when they are out of stock.

Let's look a bit deeper into these options and how they work with your Amazon listings:

Shopify Will Track Your Inventory

If you opt for this, Shopify updates Amazon listings automatically so the total product inventory stored in Shopify is matched.

Shopify Will Not Track Inventory

If the inventory policy for any product is set as Don't Track, Shopify ensures that the product is always available on Amazon. The Amazon Seller Central account will show inventory as 100 for the product, but this will not appear in Shopify.

Amazon provides no support for unlimited quantities of products so you need to use 100 as a placeholder. Although it will decrease as products sell, every 10 minutes it will be updated back to 100.

Customers May Purchase Products When They Are Out of Stock

If you opt to allow customers to purchase when something is out of stock, Shopify ensures that the same product is available on Amazon. Again, the inventory is set as 100 for Amazon but won't appear in Shopify.

Important Note - Success on Amazon relied largely on positive reviews from your customers so do not sell stock on Amazon that is not available- people are very quick to leave negative reviews!

- Your final step is to get selling. Any orders made on Amazon sync automatically with the orders page on your Shopify store. Any new Amazon orders will show in your Orders list and will be marked as being Amazon sales accordingly. All orders are synced by Shopify, including those for products that have only been listed on Amazon.

- Customers will get their order notifications only from Amazon while you get them from Shopify too. If the order is not fulfilled through Shopify, it won't be updated.

Integrating Amazon and Shopify is easier than it looks and you won't regret doing it. Sales should receive a significant boost as your audience and target market is considerably wider.

BONUS CHAPTER

SHOPIFY AND FACEBOOK

As well as Amazon, it can greatly benefit you to integrate your Shopify store with your Facebook account, and any other social media account you have, Not only does this vastly improve the quality of your store, it also makes it more convenient for users and potentially boosts sales.

Some parts of the integration will make it far easier for you to advertise your store quickly and with less energy expended! Two examples are Facebook shop extensions and dynamic ads, which we'll talk about later. Other parts of the integration help to boost engagement with your store, build up trust with your customers and boost your sales. These are all benefits that you really can't afford to ignore if you want true success with your Shopify store.

Let's get started.

SHOPIFY

The first step is to install the Tracing Pixel provided by Facebook in your Shopify store. This pixel has two advantages – it tracks the activity of your users which allows you to use Facebook ads to retarget users and it also lets you know whether your Facebook ads are proving to be effective by providing details on clicks that result in conversions.

You don't need to have any coding experience to install the pixel as Shopify pretty much does it all for you. Here's how:

1. In your Facebook account, go to All Tools > Measure and Report > Pixels

2. Copy your Pixel ID number (write it down or highlight and copy)

3. Now go to your Shopify store and click on "Online Store."

4. Click on "Preferences" and go to the tab for "Facebook Pixel

5. Type in or paste your Pixel ID number – that's all you need to do and your pixel will be running immediately.

Using this method of installation, the tracking pixel will track these conversions automatically, with no coding required:

- AddPaymentInfo
- AddToCart
- InitiateCheckout
- Purchase

- Search
- ViewContent

The next step is to create and/or sync a Facebook shop with your Shopify store. Every business has the capacity to create Facebook shops where products can be directly sold via Facebook. If you have a Shopify Store, you can easily create a shop on Facebook that will sync with your Shopify store. This gives you two platforms for selling your products on and any inventory in Shopify is automatically updated to your Facebook shop at the time it updates on Shopify. You could, as you can with Amazon, choose to sell certain products on Facebook only and not have them show up in your Shopify store.

The best way to create your shop is to use the Facebook app in the Shopify store. It is a free app, but you must be using a paid package, as an absolute minimum, the $9 per month Lite Plan. Install the app and then, to set the shop up, you need your Facebook page connected.

If you have goods online already, Facebook reviews the shop and this can take up to two days to complete. Once Facebook has passed the review, your Shop can be enabled so goods can be published on Facebook.

You can also allow your customers the choice of checking out their cart on Shopify or, if their payment is in USD, to checkout using Facebook.

Next, dynamic ads can be set up. Don't avoid this step as you can use these ads to target customers who already looked at specific products on your site. Again, no coding is required because you

SHOPIFY

can use an app to set the ads up and use the Pixel that you installed earlier:

- Go to the Shopify app store and get an app called Facebook Product Feed – the developer is Flexify. Once you install it, choose which products to include in the feed – to select a product it must be visible in your store.

- Next, click on "Native Shopify Pixel Setting" and choose "Format Feed."

- Copy the feed URL from the top of the page and go back to your Ads Manager on Facebook

- Click All Tools > Assets > Catalogs

- Creating a new catalog requires you to choose the product category so go ahead and do that and then choose which page your catalog will belong to and give the catalog a name

- Click on "Add Products"

- Choose how your data feed is going to be uploaded – click on "Set a Schedule" and input the feed URL you copied earlier. If you have a password protecting the feed, input the information

- Lastly, decide how to update the feed – hourly or weekly is best for dynamic ads

Your product feed is now ready and you can start running those dynamic ads.

Now, what we want to do next is choose to feature UGC in your Shopify store. UGC is User Generated Content and this goes a long way towards helping boost your sales. Much of this comes down to your visitors tending to trust people more than brands so, by adding a very prominent UGC that comes from your own social feeds, you can boost sales significantly.

There are a few Shopify as that can help you, including:

- Contentplum – 15-day free trial, $19.99 minimum per month

- Pixlee for Shopify- custom pricing

- Socialphotos – 30-day free trial, $10-$15 per month

Important Tip

By adding your social media accounts to your store, you are providing potential customers with a way of gaining access to your community online. This makes for a better relationship and lets visitors see information about your store before you go ahead and make a purchase.

There are a few apps that help you to add your social media icons to your storefront and these take visitors to each of your social accounts. One of the best free apps is called Social Media Tabs and, when installed in your store you can pick the icons you want on show, along with the icon color and their location in the store.

SHOPIFY

Don't ignore the power of Facebook and other social media accounts when it comes to boosting sales. Social media has the ability to reach much further and much wider than any other marketing strategy you might think of and they have been proven as effective and efficient ways to promote a business. Many of the top brands spend time and money on keeping their social media accounts up to date and to integrate with your Shopify account will maximize all the benefits you can gain.

CONCLUSION

Thanks for choosing this guide to read, I hope that it provided a helpful insight into how to set up and use Shopify to make money. You should now have a pretty good understanding of what Shopify is and what it can do for you.

It doesn't matter whether you are selling a few items to make money through a blog, are setting up a huge online store or even adding an online angle to your physical business, Shopify is the store to be in, offering plenty of tools and support to help you get your store up and running and be a success.

I hope that you are now ready to join the 'gold-rush' and choose Shopify as your way forward. It doesn't cost much to do and you can start small and see how things pan out before you make the leap and go big. If it doesn't work you haven't lost much so you really don't have anything to lose.

It will work though, provided you put the effort in and go for it.

Thank you for taking the time to read this guide and I wish you all the best in your Shopify venture.

DROPSHIPPING

A BEGINNER'S GUIDE TO MAKING MONEY ONLINE

BY BRETT STANDARD

INTRODUCTION

Congratulations on purchasing *Dropshipping: A Beginner's Guide to Making Money Online* and thank you for doing so.

The following chapters will discuss the dropshipping business model, and they will give you all the information that you will need to start your first dropshipping store and to operate it successfully. From this book, you will be able to learn in detail on how dropshipping works, what the advantages of the business model are, what challenges you are likely to deal with if you venture into the dropshipping business, and what you need to do to start your own dropshipping business.

This book will take you through all the specific steps that you will have to follow as you establish your business, and it will point out all the pitfalls that you should avoid in your journey to success. You will get a lot of insider tips on how to find a niche and how to identify great products. You will also learn how to find great reliable suppliers and the best ways to set up your order fulfillment process.

This guide also provides a lot of practical advice on how to run your business and how to scale it to make it more profitable. It will also provide you with procedural information as well as tips and tricks with regards to running your dropshipping business on marketplaces such as Shopify, Amazon, and eBay. Finally, it will discuss how you can avoid some of the common mistakes that new drop-shippers tend to make.

There are lots of books on dropshipping in the market right now, so thank you very much for selecting this one! Every effort was made to ensure that this book is full of useful and actionable information, so please enjoy!

CHAPTER 1 –

HOW DOES THE DROPSHIPPING MODEL WORK?

Dropshipping is a fairly new branch of e-commerce where entrepreneurs buy and sell goods directly to the customers without having to put up huge amounts of capital and without having to hold onto large amounts of inventory. Most people who hear about dropshipping for the first time find the notion a bit confusing, but in actual sense, it's pretty simple to grasp.

If you are in this business, all you have to do is find people who are willing to buy certain goods, find suppliers who are selling those goods, purchase the goods from the suppliers at a lower price, sell it to the buyers at a higher price, then pocket the difference. What's more, you can ship the product directly from your suppliers to your customers, so you don't have to hold onto inventory at any given time.

The concept itself is that simple—the execution, however, is much more complicated.

The main difference between traditional retail practice and dropshipping is that you as an entrepreneur or a merchant don't have to stock up or even to own inventory at any given time. All you have to do is buy as much inventory as you need and exactly when you need it, from someone else who sells in bulk. Once you have received an order from a customer, you can buy from a wholesaler or even directly from the manufacturer of the product in order to fulfill that order. This model allows you to stay liquid at all times because you don't ever have to invest your money on the stock. You just have to wait until you have received a payment from a customer, and then pay a certain fraction of that payment to the supplier to cover the product and shipping costs.

In e-commerce textbooks, dropshipping is referred to as a "supply chain management method," and it can be used in both online and brick and mortar stores, but the concept has become more popular with the rise of e-commerce because it's much more viable as a model for online stores. Just like in ordinary retail businesses, the profit margin that you have to work with as a drop-shipper is the difference between the wholesale price and the retail price of the product that you are selling.

Here Is How the Dropshipping Model Works

To start a dropshipping business, the first thing you need to do is to find a product that you want to sell. This first part is really challenging because there are already thousands of other dropshipping companies online that are already up and running, so you can't just wake up one day and start selling a certain product—you may find it hard to compete with someone who has already developed trust with customers. What you need to do is to find a niche and to brainstorm ways to differentiate yourself from other retailers.

Finding the right niche for your dropshipping business isn't easy—it requires you to do a lot of research. You need to identify an area where you may be able to fill a market gap, where you may be able to create added value (either by providing products that are slightly better or by providing valuable information to go along with those products), where you can provide products that are difficult to find locally, or where you can provide products that are slightly more affordable than those of your competitors.

After you have a niche, you have to find a supplier for your product(s). There are specific characteristics of a good supplier that you will have to look out for. First, the supplier has to be one who is willing to drop-ship. There are some suppliers who may frown upon the idea of having to sell their products through you as a middle-man, so you should find out early enough if they work with drop-shippers to avoid wasting your time on them. Other wholesale suppliers may be unwilling to break their large batches of products in order to send out orders one by one. You need to look far and wide to find a supplier who has the capacity to fulfill all your customers' orders, and one whose business model is optimized for dropshipping.

Next, you have to correspond with your suppliers to make sure that they meet your requirements in terms of shipping methods, shipping times, quality control, prices, etc. For your dropshipping business to work, your supplier must be completely reliable, and the relationship between you two must be built on solid ground.

Most wholesalers who work with dropshipping businesses keep a roster which you will have to join. In order to join a wholesaler's or supplier's roster, you have to provide details about your business, and in many cases, you may have to pay a membership fee.

You have to identify specific products that you will be selling and make sure that your supplier has a sizable stock of that product, and then you have to set up an account with that supplier. You may find that there are many variations of a particular product, but there are specific variations that do particularly well in the market. Even if you have already decided on a niche, you should take time to do a bit of market research before you pick specific makes and models of the product.

Setting up an account with a supplier may require you to provide some documentation to prove that you are a legitimate business entity, and you may have to sign some documents that are provided by the supplier. The supplier may need to see applicable business licenses from you, and the two of you may have to come to an agreement on terms such as payment rates, methods, and schedules. You may have to sign a binding contract in some cases.

Dropshipping businesses are enterprises like any others, so they have to be structured as legally recognizable entities. You may have to register your dropshipping business as a company, a proprietorship, or a corporation, depending on your own personal preferences and on the volume of business that you want to transact through it. If the law requires your dropshipping company to have certain licenses, ensure that you acquire them. Dropshipping businesses also need to be registered for federal tax—you may use your own social security number for tax purposes if you have a proprietorship, but you have to get a tax ID if you have used other legal structures for the business.

Dropshipping businesses are either run on specific e-commerce platforms or on standalone e-commerce websites. If you are looking to start a dropshipping business, you have to choose between selling your products in an existing marketplace and actually creating your own online store.

If you choose to sell your products in a marketplace that already exists, you may run a risk of being overshadowed by multiple other sellers who have products that are similar to yours. If you choose to set up your own e-commerce shop, you can use a service that helps you create your shop, or you can opt to purchase your own domain name and set up your online shop from scratch. Every option comes with its own challenges, but the best choice for you would be to diversify. It's better to get listed in multiple platforms and marketplaces in order to reach the largest possible pool of customers.

DROPSHIPPING

If you want to build your own website for your dropshipping business, you have to find a secure and reliable hosting service and a great domain name for your business. If you have decent web design skills, put them to use and create a unique and captivating website. If you can't do web design, hire a trustworthy professional designer to do it for you. You will need a merchant account that is built into your website along with a shopping cart to allow you to make sells. If you are selling on a marketplace that already exists (e.g. Amazon, eBay, etc.), you will need to sign up for an account under the "seller" category.

Dropshipping businesses need to set up the necessary digital infrastructure to accept payments, so as you list yourself in various marketplaces, or as you create your own e-commerce website, set up a system where you can receive payments by credit card, PayPal, or any other means. You may also have to provide your customers with a toll-free number where they can call you or an email address through which they can contact you in case they have any problems with your product.

Listing products on your website or on your page in an online marketplace isn't that complicated. Most suppliers and wholesalers make it easy for drop-shippers to just copy and paste pictures of the products that they want to sell. Wholesalers also provide detailed descriptions of their products which you can copy-paste, modify, and post on your website alongside the pictures. In order to differentiate yourself from other retailers, you may want to come up with your own unique content for the description on your website instead of just copying whatever the wholesaler provides.

For your dropshipping business to work, you have to get your pricing just right. If you choose to price your products too low, you may not be able to generate enough of a profit to make your efforts worthwhile. If you set your prices too high, you may not be able to compete with other retailers who are selling similar products at a more affordable price. To set the right price, consider what you are paying the supplier, what the supplier is charging you for shipping, and what percentage of profit you intend to make. If you are lucky enough to find a rare product that is on high demand, you may be able to make high percentages of profits. However, with most products, your best option will be to keep your prices close or similar to wholesaler's recommended retail price. That's because most other retailers will do the same, and you will be at a disadvantage if you tried to price your products differently.

The dropshipping model may also work for auction sites (e.g. eBay). You can list your products as new, set a minimum price for the product, and start your bidding countdown clock. If you are using an auction website to sale your dropshipping products, ensure that at the very least, the minimum bid should cover the cost of the product plus shipping to avoid making losses. The remainder of the process is the same as it is for non-auction sites—you have to send the product directly from the supplier to the winner's address after they have made the payment.

When it comes to shipping, a dropshipping business should have clear shipping and return policies that customers are made to understand from the very beginning. If you want to set up your business in an existing marketplace, make sure that you understand and comply with any of the shipping rules of that marketplace and make sure that you convey the same rules to your customers.

After everything is set up, all you have to do is market your store and wait for someone to purchase your products. There are lots of online marketing techniques that you can deploy. You should create a mailing list of all your customers so that you may be able to drum up some repeat business from them. You can send out updates about new products, promotions, and other offers. You can use social media marketing techniques, blogs, online videos, and other internet marketing methods to bring in customers. Driving traffic to your sales page isn't easy, but it's a skill that anyone can perfect with a bit of hard work and determination. You can also offer special sales, contests, and other promotions in order to pique the interest of potential customers and to increase your sales.

The moment a customer makes a purchase, you have to act immediately by turning around and ordering that exact same product from your wholesaler. The minute you verify that the customer has paid for his or her order, you should go ahead and relay it to the supplier. Try to avoid delays at all costs, because the last thing you want is to fail to deliver to your customer on time.

In order to save time, you should have a notification system in place so that you know about order placements when they happen. If you can afford to, hire one or more people to act on customer orders in real time. Pay the supplier and instruct him to ship the product to the customer's address. If the supplier provides you with a tracking number for your shipment, use it to monitor the shipment and ensure that everything is on schedule.

The customers also need to know about the progress of their shipments, so set up a mechanism where they can be automatically notified once the shipment is sent out. After you have closed the sale, send them subsequent emails telling them when their products have been shipped, and when they can expect to receive them. Be available to pick up calls and to address their concerns in case any problems arise.

For the dropshipping business to work, you will need to have open lines of communication with your suppliers so that you can find solutions to problems as soon as possible. The shipping process has many inherent risks—products may break during transit, and you may need to replace them in the shortest time possible. In some cases, you may have problems with your supplier—he may either fail to send out your product on time, or he may run out of stock.

As a retailer, your reputation depends on your ability to deliver on your shipment on time. The problem of back ordering occurs rather frequently with some suppliers, especially those who service multiple retailers. If your supplier runs out of stock, you may be unable to fulfill a customer's order, and you may be forced to cancel on him, which could reflect poorly on you if the customers chose to complain about your service delivery online or to give you a negative rating or review.

You have to take measures to prevent a situation where you are forced to cancel orders because your supplier is out of stock. It may be in your best interest to build some redundancy into your system by having more than one supplier so that if the main one is unable to deliver for any reason, you may order your product from your backup supplier.

As a dropshipping retailer, it's absolutely crucial that you keep the fact that you are sourcing your product somewhere else hidden from both your current and your prospective customers. The survival of your business depends on people believing that you are the best source of whatever product they are looking for. If they discover that you are sourcing your product from a third party and selling it to them, they may opt to cut you out of the whole process and try to buy the product from the supplier by themselves.

In order to conceal your suppliers from your customers, you have to practice what is known as "blind shipping." This is a process where you ship your products without including a return address on the package or a receipt from the supplier. Remember that in dropshipping, the product goes directly from your supplier to your customer. If the supplier puts a receipt inside the package, the customer will notice that the supplier's name is different from your business name, and he may decide to Google the supplier and order from him the next time he wants something.

A common alternative to "blind shipping" is called "private label shipping." This is where the product is shipped directly from the supplier to the customer, but instead of listing the supplier's address as the return address, a customized slip from the retailer is stuck onto the package. The customized slip would contain the retailer's logo and contact information so that if the customer had a problem with his shipment, he would contact the retailer and ask for a way forward rather than sending the package back. Most major suppliers who work with dropshipping retailers will allow you to create a customized package slip if you choose to practice "private label shipping."

For your dropshipping business to work correctly, the final thing that you have to do is to follow up on your customers to ensure that they are satisfied after their purchase orders have been delivered. If customers have any complaints that are specific to your product (e.g. its quality, how it's packaged, or how it's delivered), make sure that you address those concerns to their satisfaction and that you learn from them to improve your services. At the end of the day, dropshipping works best if there is a personal touch to your service delivery.

At face value, dropshipping may seem like an easy process that anyone can wake up one day and start doing, but that's not the case. For you to succeed in this business, you must be deliberate, dedicated, and determined. Like any other low-risk business, dropshipping has attracted many entrepreneurs, and because of the resulting competition, the business has become less lucrative and harder to break into than it was a few years ago. That doesn't mean that it's no longer a viable business model. It just means that if you want to succeed, you have to be more pragmatic in your approach to the business.

Don't go into dropshipping with unrealistic expectations of making super-normal profits overnight. Instead, you should take your time to study the market and to identify products whose profitability you can predict with a level of certainty. Your decision to market and sell a certain product shouldn't be based on hype. Instead, it should be based on the analysis of market data, which can clearly tell you if there is a viable market for that product.

CHAPTER 2 –

THE ADVANTAGES OF STARTING A DROPSHIPPING BUSINESS

There are many advantages of starting a dropshipping company, but in order to benefit from those advantages, make sure that you understand how the dropshipping model works and ensure that you stick to the model.

All retail businesses are inherently risky, but many of the risks of ordinary retail and e-commerce businesses are somewhat mitigated in the dropshipping model because they don't fall within your docket as a drop-shipper—most risks are borne by third-party suppliers. A lot of the advantages of dropshipping stem from the fact that you as an entrepreneur are at liberty to try things out without having to risk too much.

Here are some of the major benefits of investing in a dropshipping business:

Less Startup Capital Investment Compared to Other Models

One of the most important advantages of dropshipping is that you can launch your business without needing to put down a lot of money into purchasing inventory. That means that pretty much anyone can start a dropshipping business. Even if you are a broke student or someone without access to much capital, you won't be locked out of this business.

In traditional retail businesses, before you are able to start your shop you have to spend thousands of dollars stocking up on inventory without any guarantee that you will be able to offload any of it. For most people, starting a traditional retail business would mean taking a bank loan, or using a huge chunk (if not all) of their savings on inventory. However, with dropshipping, if you are savvy enough, you could get your business off the ground with almost zero capital investment.

In dropshipping, you never have to purchase a product until you have made a sale, and the customer has already paid you. It's like being an agent who makes a commission by selling a supplier's product to a customer without having to put his own money down. In fact, when you are getting started, the only investment you absolutely have to make will go into setting up your online shop, registering with suppliers, and marketing your brand to increase visibility—none of your money has to go into production costs.

The agreements that people make with suppliers tend to vary, but the one constant is that you don't have to make an upfront payment for your products. If you find a supplier who insists that you to pay for his product in bulk, you should know that he is not the right supplier for your dropshipping business, and you should keep looking around until you find one who is suitable for this model.

Low Overhead Costs

Apart from spending a lot of money on inventory, running a traditional retail business would require you to spend a fortune on overhead expenses, most of which you don't have to worry about if you decide to try out dropshipping. In traditional e-commerce businesses, you would have to rent offices, warehouses, and transportation vehicles. If you were importing your own products, you would have to pay ocean freight fees, and spend a lot of cash hiring warehouse workers to store, sort, package, and distribute your products. It would mean that you'd have to pay for rent, utilities, insurance costs, transportation costs, maintenance costs, etc.

Many traditional retail businesses fail because they end up buried in unforeseen overhead expenses. In dropshipping, you never have to worry about any of the logistical issues and the overhead expenses. You don't have to be concerned about paying warehouse workers, being late on utility bills or not being able to make enough for rent that month. Most people run their dropshipping businesses from their homes (although if you find it necessary, you can rent a small office from which to run your operations).

Whenever you have an order to fulfill, you essentially outsource all the duties that are involved in the process to a third party, all at a bargained cost that is manageable. Your supplier will have to deal with storing your products in a warehouse, organizing and packaging the products before shipment, labeling them properly, shipping them, tracking them, and delivering them to your customers. The supplier will give you the tracking number for each product so that you can keep tabs on it, but you don't require many resources to do that. The only cost that is absolutely necessary, is the cost of operating a customer service line (preferably one that is toll-free).

Easy for You to Get Started

Starting a traditional e-commerce retail business requires a lot of technical know-how that just isn't necessary when it comes to dropshipping. When you run a dropshipping business, you don't have to spend a lot of time learning every single detail about how to operate and manage warehouses, how to hire warehouse employees, and how to provide them with a safe working environment. You never have to learn what goes into packing and shipping your products, let alone what goes into manufacturing them. You never have to learn the intricacies of optimal inventory management. You don't have to learn the accounting mathematics that goes into tracking products through different parts of the supply chain. All you have to do is find a reliable supplier who will do all of those things for you, and you will already be in business.

Can be Highly Scalable

If you run a traditional business, you would have to increase the amount of work that you had to do if the number of orders that you received was to increase significantly. However, with dropshipping, that doesn't have to be the case. The only work you have to do is to relay the shipping order from the customer to the manufacturer, so you won't be burdened with the responsibility of having to hire extra workers to increase your production. That means that once you have set up your dropshipping business to process a given number of orders every day, the only thing you have to do to scale up by any factor is to increase your capacity to receive and submit orders, which is neither difficult nor technical.

If your sales grow significantly, the only people you will need to hire to meet the increase in demand will be customer service people. A traditional retail business that finds itself in a similar situation will have to hire more warehouse workers, purchase more packaging materials, hire more managers, construct more facilities and warehouses, and invest more on transportation. In dropshipping, none of those things will stand in your way when you want to scale up.

Dropshipping is also highly scalable when you want to upgrade the quality of the product that you are selling. The effort that it takes to drop-ship an item that costs $1 is the same effort that it will take you to drop-ship an item that costs $1000. That means that if you want to switch from selling cheap items to expensive items, you won't have to exert any more effort than you already do. By contrast, if you wanted to switch from a cheaper product to a more expensive one in a traditional retail business, you would have to invest a lot of money into upgrading your production capacity. With dropshipping, nothing changes—you just relay the customers' orders to the suppliers as you have always done. If you want to scale up by adding new products to your online shop, all you have to do is find the right product and supplier, market test it, and add it to your shop.

An increase in the number of customer orders may cause you to run out of stock more often, but that is not a hindrance to scalability. If your customer base grows, you can always increase the number of suppliers that you have in order to meet the extra demand.

You Can Do It from Any Location

If you have a dropshipping business that is already operational, you have the flexibility to run it from pretty much anywhere you want, as long as you have an internet connection. The supplier will deal with every physical aspect of your business, leaving you to handle only the digital stuff, which doesn't restrict you to a given location. When you are setting up your business for the first time, you may need to stay grounded because you may have to acquire things like permits, a tax ID, licenses, etc. (some of these things can also be done online). However, the minute that you have all things set up, the only obligation you will have is to be able to stay in communication with your suppliers and your customers.

As part of your due diligence, while you are still establishing your business, you may have to visit your suppliers' facilities to verify that they indeed have the capacity to provide the product you are looking for on a consistent basis. However, beyond that, the business doesn't require you to be physically present at any one place. Some people have been able to operate profitable dropshipping businesses while on vacation in exotic locations, or while trotting around the globe.

If you choose to travel as you run your dropshipping business, you can easily communicate with your suppliers and customers through email. However, if you prefer talking to them over the phone, it's important to remember that international or cross-country phone calls can be rather expensive, and they may put a significant dent on your bottom-line.

Ensures a High Customer Lifetime Value

In business and marketing, the term "customer lifetime value" is used to refer to the amount of net profit that a business can generate thanks to its relationship with a particular customer throughout the remainder of his or her life. Dropshipping gives you the ability to increasingly expand your selection of products by adding new ones to your online store whenever you want to. This makes it possible for you to keep your customers interested enough so that they will want to return again and make other purchases in the future. This works best when you have found a niche that is unique, and you have curated a product line around that niche in a way that your competitors haven't been able to do.

Minimizes Your Risk

Traditional retail businesses come with lots of inherent risks, some of which cannot be mitigated against. If you put your money into a traditional business, there is always the chance that your product won't move, and you will be stuck with useless inventory. If you operate your own warehouses, there are risks such as accidents, fires, water damage, among others. If you ship your own goods, there are risks of breakages, damages, and lost packages. When you run a dropshipping operation, you won't have to shoulder any of those risks.

If you are selling trendy products, there is always the possibility that trends will change, and people's tastes will be different in a few weeks or months. What if you sank all your capital into the inventory of that product? Well, with dropshipping, that is not something you ever have to worry about. Even if you invest in a certain niche product only to find out that its sales volumes are lower than you had expected, you can always pivot to another product without losing too much capital (your only loss will be the cash you put into creating your website and doing some marketing).

Enables You to Come to Market a lot Quicker

If you are familiar with the term "opportunity cost," you understand that any delays to get to market can technically be considered as loses. If there are two people looking to start e-commerce retail businesses, the one who chooses dropshipping will get started almost immediately, while the one who chooses a traditional e-commerce model will have to spend a lot of time looking for capital, learning the intricacies of the business and setting things up before he can finally enter the market. By the time the other guy official launches his business, the one who took the dropshipping route will already be making money.

Another aspect of this is how long it takes to ship products in traditional e-commerce versus how long it takes to do the same in dropshipping. In traditional e-commerce, you first have to ship the product from the supplier to your own facilities, then you have to ship the same product again from your warehouses to the client. It takes a lot more time for the product to reach the customer in traditional e-commerce than it does in dropshipping and that time difference matters a lot. If the product is a trendy one that could go out of fashion at any given time, the entrepreneur who chooses the dropshipping model will get into the market fast enough, make a killing, then get out before the trend changes. The other guy will get into the market a little much later, and he'd be stuck with outdated inventory if things change.

Sell an Unlimited Selection of Products

There is no limit to the variety of products that you can sell through the dropshipping model. You don't have to own or physically possess whatever you are selling. All you have to do is list it on your website or sales page to find out if there is anyone who is willing to buy it. That means that you can list as many products as you want, and you won't lose anything by doing that. On the other hand, traditional e-commerce retailers are limited to the selection of products that they already have in stock, and sometimes, they may have to hold off introducing new and trendy products because they need to clear inventory that is backlogged.

Because of the unlimited selection of products at your disposal, it's easy for you to expand into new markets. In fact, when some suppliers introduce new products, they will allow you to add them on your website for free if you are already in their roster of registered merchants.

Access to Unlimited Amounts of Inventory

There is no limit to the number of products that you can sell. If you have a good enough marketing campaign to go along with your dropshipping business, you may find yourself selling your products like hot cakes. If this happens, you never have to worry about running out of inventory because you are getting your supply directly from a supplier who keeps enough stock to service several merchants. Even if there is a likelihood that your supplier will run out, you always have the option of having backup suppliers. In theory, your inventory is virtually unlimited, so if you are well organized, you will never have to turn a customer away for any reason.

Less Time Consumed

Most of the things that you need to do to set up and to operate your dropshipping business can be done in a hassle-free and convenient way. You don't have to deal with the hassle of storing and packaging your products in preparation for shipment. All the labor-intensive parts of the job are handled by suppliers and wholesalers. You can also add new products to your sales page with just a few clicks and begin making money almost immediately. Compared to other retail models, dropshipping is indeed extremely convenient.

Less Products With Little Risk

All the time-consuming activities that are involved in the e-commerce retail process are delegated to other parties in the dropshipping model. The only thing you have to do on a day to day basis is to relay the customers' orders to the suppliers and send customers notification about the current location and the ETA of their packages. That means that you don't need to spend too much time running this type of business.

This business is, therefore, a good option not just for full-time entrepreneurs, but also for people who have other obligations. You can run a dropshipping business while you have a full-time job, a part-time job, or even as you pursue a college degree. If you have a startup e-commerce shop where you do your own packaging and shipping, your business will suffer if you split your attention and focus on other things such as a job or school.

Test Products with Little Risk

Dropshipping is the only e-commerce retail model where you can get to test the viability of different products in the market without risking too much of your capital. In fact, lots of experienced drop-shippers do exactly that. They list products in their websites and sales pages, and they wait to see if there is any market out there for those products. If after a while there is no visible enthusiasm for the product, they pull it off their list of offerings and try a different product altogether, until they find the one that generates the most profit. That kind of trial and error approach isn't a viable technique in any other model of e-commerce. If you put money into inventory that doesn't sell, you can say bye to your capital.

Increases Your Favorability with Wholesalers

Wholesalers love dropshipping businesses because they expand and boost their sales to levels that were previously unimaginable. Before dropshipping came along, obscure manufacturers and wholesalers had to rely on big stores and e-commerce websites alone to get their products to the consumer, and even then, it was hard for some of those products to receive any visibility online or even in physical stores. When dropshipping came along, it changed the game for wholesalers because they now have the ability to sell more goods and to reach wider customer bases.

Wholesalers look favorably upon dropshipping businesses, and some of them have been going out of their way to make their products and services available to drop-shippers. Dropshippers and wholesalers have relationships that are mutually beneficial, and if you start a dropshipping business, you too can benefit from those relationships.

CHAPTER 3 –

THE DISADVANTAGES OF STARTING A DROPSHIPPING BUSINESS

Like many other business models, dropshipping has its share of disadvantages, most of which we will be discussing in this chapter. You have already seen some of the advantages of dropshipping, and as you read about the disadvantages, you will realize that some of them are direct results of the advantages that we discussed earlier. Some of the things that make dropshipping attractive to many merchants also have the effect of making it harder for individual merchants to succeed as drop-shippers. In other words, some of the positive incentives that attract people into these businesses have a way of turning into "perverse incentives" and ruining the viability of many dropshipping niches.

We are not discussing the disadvantages of dropshipping in order to scare you away from this model. Instead, we are outlining all the things that could go wrong with your dropshipping business so that you can know what to expect, and you can understand what you need to do to mitigate against any problems that may arise. We will be doing you a disservice if we only talked about the positive aspects of dropshipping without informing you about its negative aspects. If you fully understand common problems that drop-shippers face, you will be better equipped to distinguish yourself, to rise above the fray, and to succeed in your business.

Here are some of the disadvantages that you may have to deal with as you run your dropshipping business:

Low-Profit Margins

The biggest disadvantage that you would have to deal with in the dropshipping business is the low-profit margins. It's extremely easy to get started in this business and that has attracted many entrepreneurs, and it has made most niches very competitive. There are hundreds or even thousands of merchants who are willing to start online shops and to sell their products at a very small profit margin, so every new entrant into the game has to keep his or her prices close to those of everyone else in order to stay competitive.

The vast majority of dropshipping merchants build low-quality sites, and they barely offer any customer service, so their operating costs are low. When customers are looking for the product that you are selling, they now have online tools that will help them compare your product prices to those of other similar products, so even if you have a good marketing strategy, you have no choice but to set your prices low in order to make any sales.

The low-profit margin also results from the fact that drop-shippers don't get to purchase their product as a wholesale or "bulk" price because they sell their products one item at a time. Compared to a traditional e-commerce shop that carries its own inventory, drop-shippers have to pay more per item, so at the end of the day, their profit margins are limited.

Wholesalers are right to charge drop-shippers more than other merchants because they go through a lot of trouble to package each item individually rather than sending out bulk orders. This costs them more in terms of packaging material, labor, and transportation costs, so they feel the need to transfer those costs to the owner of the dropshipping business.

The profit that you make as a retailer in the dropshipping business is your selling price minus all other costs, including the cost of buying from the supplier, shipping costs, and your own operating costs (e.g. the amount you pay for ads and content development). If you already have less than a 20% margin to work with after subtracting the supplier's charge, you can end up with a really minuscule profit margin.

In order to make decent profits as a drop-shipper, you have to move high volumes of the product. You can also do a lot of research in order to identify a niche that works well with the dropshipping model. We will be discussing how to find a great niche later in this book.

Suppliers Are Prone to Making Human Errors

Dropshipping suppliers tend to service a lot of merchants, and because of the high volumes of the orders that they have to fulfill, they often end up making human errors. If you have chosen to work with the cheapest supplier as a way to cut your costs, chances are that he would end up making frequent mistakes which the customers will end up blaming on you because they are doing business with you, and not your supplier.

If the supplier fails to keep his stock levels up, you may end up accepting orders from customers only to find out that your supplier is unable to fulfill them. Whenever there are bungled shipments or missing packages, you will have no choice but to take responsibility for the errors. You can mitigate against some of the human errors by having backup suppliers and backups to the backups so that if one supplier fails, you don't have to let down your customer and come across as unprofessional.

Issues with Inventory

Compared to traditional e-commerce businesses that stock their own inventory, dropshipping means that you have no idea how much stock is actually available at any given time, so you have to source your products from multiple suppliers to avoid a scenario where you run out of stock. However, even that solution presents its own problems with your inventory. Some technological solutions are available to help owners of dropshipping businesses sync up their sales records with their suppliers' stock records, but most suppliers don't invest in support systems for such technologies because they aren't the primary benefactors of such technologies. Technological solutions also fall short because it's hard to project the suppliers' inventory depletion rate since they service multiple dropshipping businesses at the same time.

Shipping Costs Can Get Complicated

Many drop-shippers work with multiple suppliers at any given time, and this opens up the opportunity for shipping costs to get really complicated and unnecessarily high. Take the example of a customer who orders a handful of items from your dropshipping business. If you source each item from a different warehouse, you will have to pay a shipping fee for each of the items that the customer receives. You will have a difficult time convincing a customer who has checked out multiple items in one cart that there is a shipping cost attached to each individual item—customers who are used to shipping deals from places like Amazon may find that ridiculous. They'll assume you are trying to grossly overcharge them for shipping, and they may even decide not to buy your products anymore. If you choose to offset the shipping costs on your end, you may find yourself actually making a loss on that sale! In a scenario such as this one, it's impossible for you to come out on top.

Competition

Because it's easy to get started, there are many people who have set up dropshipping businesses, and while this is a good thing for the consumer, it is a very big challenge for you if you want to succeed as a drop-shipper. You can find that hundreds of people are selling the same exact product, so it makes it hard for any one person to break out from the crowd and to make extraordinary amounts of profits. In many cases, you even have to go up against juggernauts like Walmart or Amazon who won't hesitate to undercut smaller retailers whenever they feel like it. When the profit margin is already low, you have very little room to outmaneuver dozens if not hundreds of competitors.

Shipping Can Be Slow

Marketing research shows that shipping time is one of the main factors that most online shoppers consider when they are looking to make a purchase decision. When you drop-ship your customers' orders, you don't have any control over the logistics of your shipments, which means that you can't optimize shipping times. You just have to rely on your supplier's shipping speed and hope that he always keeps it up. If you had a traditional e-commerce retail shop where you do your own shipping, you would be able to provide your customers with a lot more shipping options, and you would be able to offer them guarantees when it comes to delivery times.

Suppliers aren't particularly keen on going out of their way to make fast deliveries. Faster shipping times mean additional costs for suppliers, so they are contented to do the bare minimum. At the same time, giant retailers like Amazon are doing everything in their power to cut down their shipping times, so it makes it very hard for drop-shippers to compete. Even if a supplier offers tiered delivery services at different costs, as a drop-shipper, you may find it hard to select the fastest and most expensive package because it would affect your profit margin which is already small, to begin with.

Lack Adequate Product Information

In any e-commerce retail business, customers are always going to be asking questions about the product, and unless you can provide satisfactory answers to their queries, you could end up losing their business. The problem, however, is that dropshippers often don't get all the product information that they need from their suppliers or the manufacturers of the products. You never get to handle the product, so you can't come up with your own observations, and you can only rely on what the manufacturer tells you. Even if you understand what your product does and how it works, customers may want to know how much it weighs, what its exact physical dimensions are, and whether or not it's easy to use.

The solution to this problem might be to keep forwarding the questions that you receive from your customers to the manufacturer, but it may take a while for the manufacturer or even the supplier to get back to you, and your customer might have despaired by that time. If you choose to provide unverified information about the product on your website or social media pages, you could end up misguiding your clients, and this will be bad for your reputation.

Also, even in a case where you get all the information that you need from the manufacturer, and you copy it directly onto your dropshipping website, search engines like Google could flag you for having duplicate content on your website, and this could have a negative impact on your search engine optimization, which will, in turn, affect your online visibility and therefore your sales.

You have to deal with the risk that results from things that are out of your control

In dropshipping, you only have control over the digital aspects of your business, and you have zero control over its physical aspects. That means that you have to make commitments when you have no real way of making sure that your supplier will follow through with all your conditions. In many cases, your suppliers and wholesalers may be from a different part of the world, and they may not share your high standards when it comes to things like packaging, product handling, or even adhering to set deadlines. With all the things that are out of your hand, you run a risk of losing customers every time you fail to deliver on your promises.

The Quality of Customer Service Is Beyond Your Control

As we have already mentioned, you can't guarantee the quality of your product and the delivery process if you can't oversee how your product is made, packaged, shipped and delivered. That raises a real problem for you when it comes to delivering quality customer service. When a customer calls to inquire about the ETA of their order, the best you can do is to relay the information that your supplier gives you. When your product arrives when its late, damaged, or if the items are mixed up, the customer will call you to express his displeasure and take out his anger on you. You can try to sound apologetic, but there is no way you can offer an absolute guarantee that the issue will be fixed within the shortest time possible.

Compared to retailers who manage their own inventory and ship their own products, you can't add a personal touch to any of your products or shipment. Esthetics are important in e-commerce, and when you depend entirely on a supplier who is primarily interested in limiting his own costs, you are more likely to lose out to larger retailers who have the resources and the access to maximize the quality of the presentation of their products. Whenever any issue arises, you will find yourself stuck between a customer who is making demands and a supplier who is making excuses, and there isn't much that you can do about any of it.

Dropshipping may save you time by reducing your responsibilities, but that also limits your capacity to influence your customers' perception of your business. Since you can't have too much control over your customers' experience, you will have a big challenge when you are trying to cultivate your relationship with them and to make them more loyal to your brand. Your resolution processes for simple problems may draw out for longer than they need to, and customers may start perceiving you as unprofessional.

Pay Relatively High Fulfillment Costs

Compared to other e-commerce retailers, drop-shippers have to pay more per unit of each product that they sell. As we've mentioned, wholesalers charge drop-shippers retail prices, now wholesale prices because they ship individual products and not bulk products. Additionally, they will also charge you for shipping, packaging, and insurance. Even after accounting for all the costs, wholesalers will still add a hefty markup that will put a dent on your profit margins. Meanwhile, giant retailers such as Amazon and Walmart will only have to pay wholesale prices for their bulk purchases, which means that they stand to generate more profits if they set their final selling prices within the same ballpark as yours.

Pay-Per-Click Advertising Is Way More Expensive and Less Effective

Traditionally, the two main ways to draw traffic into your sales website have been SEO (search engine optimization) and PPC (pay-per-click). You can create optimized content for your dropshipping business to draw traffic to it, but in the past, it has been much easier to generate traffic using PPC and Google AdWords. However, because of the high number of players in the dropshipping market (and e-commerce in general), there has been an increase in demand for PPC ads, and the price of placing such ads has skyrocketed, even for niches that aren't that mainstream. With the small profit margins that drop-shippers enjoy, it has become more difficult for them to justify the cost of buying PPC ads. Given the fact that many people sell small items worth $100 or less, with a profit margin of less than 20%, buying PPC adverts could potentially wipe out more than half of one's profit margin, leaving him to pocket less than 10% of the whole deal. If you are considering buying ads, you have to decide if you are willing to make that tradeoff.

Keywords are now even more expensive than they have ever been, so instead of spending money on PPC ads, it may be wiser to invest in SEO, social media campaigns, and email solicitations. PPC may work, for you, but the risk to reward ratio seems unfavorable for most people who are trying to break into the dropshipping market.

Difficult to Brand Your Products

In a dropshipping business, you as the client have absolutely no control over how the merchandise is made, how it is packaged, how it's labeled, or even what kinds of accessories it's paired with. That makes it practically impossible for you to do any kind of branding. This shortcoming makes it quite hard for you to differentiate yourself in any way in the mind of the consumer, or to increase brand awareness and cultivate brand loyalty.

Merchants who handle their own inventory have the liberty to personalize and brand their products so that customers can get a great impression of their businesses. Suppliers tend to dropship for lots of clients, so they don't have the time to personalize the packages in any way—instead, they deliver the packages in generic low-cost boxes. Even if you were to find a supplier that is willing to brand your product for you, it would be at an additional cost that could significantly reduce your profit margin, and even then, you will have no way of verifying whether the supplier actually brands your products.

Little Control Over the Quality of Your Products

The products are made by a manufacturer that you will never get to meet. You will select them based on market analysis and niche research, but you won't be able to know if they are really of good quality, or if they are of poor quality. You don't have the ability to give the manufacturer instructions on how to make improvements, and what minimum standards he needs to meet in order to satisfy your customers. That all means that you have little to no control over the quality of the product, and you can't offer your clients any bona fide guarantees with regard to quality. That means that your brand won't be able to gain a reputation for delivering quality goods, and you would have a difficult time creating a solid customer base.

Now that we have discussed over ten disadvantages of dropshipping, the question that you may have on your mind is, "Is it worth it to invest your time and resources in a dropshipping business?"

The answer to that question is a bit complicated. As an e-commerce business model, dropshipping isn't perfect, but then again, is there any business model that is truly perfect? Even though dropshipping has lots of complex problems, you can learn to manage each and every one of those problems, and if you are more disciplined and dedicated than your competitors, you may find that in the end, you will be able to turn some disadvantages into advantages.

In the subsequent chapters, we will be providing guides on how to operate a dropshipping business, and as we do that, the solutions to some of the problems that we have discussed here will become apparent to you. By the end, you will be able to understand how to tackle each of the problems in this chapter, and this will put you at an advantage over the hundreds or even thousands of competitors that you will be up against.

CHAPTER 4 -

HOW TO START-UP THE BUSINESS

As we've mentioned, dropshipping is one of the easiest businesses to get started on because it requires little capital investment. Here is a step by step guide on how to create a dropshipping start-up.

Find a Niche

The first thing you need to do when starting a dropshipping business is to find a niche. It's difficult to compete on price alone, so having a niche will help you differentiate your business from many others, and it will give you a significant competitive advantage over your rivals.

When looking for a niche, you need to find one where you may be able to add some value, rather than just offering a generic product like every other person who is in the business. If you are passionate about a certain topic, and there is a product that goes along with it, that could be your niche. For example, if you like a certain kind of pet, you could create a blog where you post content about that pet, and you could use it to sell specific types of pet supplies that aren't commonly found everywhere else.

When looking for a niche, you need to find one with products that aren't easy to find on the local market. It's going to be difficult to break into the market if the product that you are trying to sell is already available in every corner store.

Finally, when you are looking for a niche, try to find one where the products aren't too cheap. The profit margins in dropshipping businesses are small, to begin with, so you should try to find goods that cost a bit more so that you can get a decent return for every sale that you make. Products worth $100 to $200 are ideal for this kind of business. You should try to avoid products that are too expensive because most customers would not want to purchase an expensive product unless they are able to talk to you over the phone and to receive full-time customer support.

Find Suppliers

After you have settled on a niche of your choosing, you need to identify suppliers who will be able to do the product fulfillment for you. Most people in the dropshipping business get their supplies from wholesalers, or if they are lucky, they could get the products directly from the manufacturer. When you are looking for a supplier, you shouldn't limit yourself to a few options that are commonplace. Instead, widen your net, and compare the offers that you get from all the different suppliers out there.

To find a supplier, you should do an online search of the product that you are looking for and include the word "wholesaler" in the search phrase. You will find very few wholesalers in the first few pages of Google's results because most wholesalers don't deal with customers directly, so they don't invest many resources in online advertising. That means that you may have to go through dozens of pages of search results before you find any decent prospects. You should also run a search using other key terms that are synonymous with "wholesaler." For example, you could include terms such as "resellers" or "distributors" in your search phrase.

Don't limit yourself to search engine results either. You should also look through places such as the Yellow Pages to find suppliers. You can also search for the manufacturers of the product you want, get their contact information, call them, or even visit their offices (if they are in the country) to see if they are willing to work with you. If the manufacturers can't sell your products directly, you can always ask them to put you in contact with some of their distributors. It's always a good idea to find multiple suppliers for your product, just in case there is a problem with your primary supplier.

Find a Product

After identifying suppliers who sell products within your niche, you need to go through their product listings and find the products that you think have the ability to generate a decent profit for you. You need to find out which products are popular with buyers to make sure that you enjoy a high sales volume once you get started. To identify the products that are on high demand, experts in the dropshipping business recommend that you do some market research to determine the popularity of each product that you are considering.

Market research sounds like a technical subject, but with a little training, anyone can do it. You just have to use the Google Keyword Tool to find out if the demand for a particular product is high. The keyword tool usually provides information on the total number of people that have searched for a certain product online, using either the exact product name or terms that are closely related to that product. You can also do an advanced search on eBay to find out which items experience high percentages of sales. If an item experiences 60% sales or higher, it's probably popular, and it could be a viable product for your dropshipping business.

Form a Business

Now that you know what you want to sell, how you want to sell it, and where you find a constant supply of that product, it's time to form a business. The first thing you have to do in this step is to decide what structure is ideal for your dropshipping business. You can make it a sole proprietorship, an LLC (Limited Liability Company) or a corporation. Each of the business structures comes with its own advantages and disadvantages.

A sole proprietorship is the easiest to set up because you won't have to file too much paperwork with your state (as long as you have all your tax information in order, you are good to go). The problem with a sole proprietorship is that in case there is a dispute that leads to litigation, your personal assets will be on the hook because you will be liable for any damages that your business does or any laws that it breaks.

Registering your business as an LLC will help protect you from liability. You can also choose to register your business as a corporation but that may be overkill in this situation because dropshipping businesses are supposed to be simple.

Get Permits and Licenses

After you are done registering your business, you should get all the necessary licenses and permits from the state, local, and federal authorities. You can find out what kinds of certificates you need by visiting the Small Business Administration site (sba.gov) or by making inquiries with your county government.

Most suppliers will insist that you present them with your state sales tax identification or that you show them a resale certificate issued by the state. Some states may allow you to operate without a reseller certificate but make sure that you verify your state's stipulations before you start doing any transactions.

When you have obtained the proper licenses, you should file documents with the IRS to receive a federal tax ID. Dropshipping businesses are required by law to pay federal tax, so make sure that you are always compliant and that you always keep your records straight in case you end up getting audited.

Choose a Sales Platform

There are two ways to go about it when you are choosing a sales platform. The first option is to set up your own e-commerce website, and the second option is to set your business up in a marketplace that already exists. If you want to use an existent marketplace, you need to understand that although you will have an easy time setting things up, you may have to list your business against many competitors who share that platform, and you may get lost in a crowd of dropshipping companies, which means that you will have a difficult time making sales and building a customer base.

Still, you could set up a store on eBay, Amazon, Bonanza, or other marketplaces, and you could optimize it to maximize your sales. On the other hand, if you choose to set up your own store, you could use web services such as SaleHoo to create the store, or you could purchase your own domain name, create a website, build a brand, and list your products there.

Create a Payment System

You also have to set up a payment system that will allow you to receive money from your clients and also send money to your suppliers. If you are setting up your business in an existing marketplace, you won't have to worry about payment systems because those platforms already have their own integrated payment systems, and they will automatically process all of your transactions.

If you set up your store by building your own website, you have to get a merchant account from a service provider. You will also need a payment gateway account to make it possible for you to receive credit card payments from your customers. There are several service providers in the market including CyberSource, Authorize.net, and Verisign who you can work with to create payment systems that are integrated into your e-commerce site.

Although credit card payments work just fine for dropshipping businesses, PayPal is an easier and more convenient alternative to use. PayPal provides a shopping cart function that you can add to your e-commerce site for free and use it to process payments in a quick and secure manner. Because you want to reach the largest possible customer base, it may be wise to integrate all the popular payment methods that are available out there into your system so that customers have a variety of choices when they want to check out from your store.

Set Up a Customer Service System

You should also create a customer service and communication system to allow you to talk to both your customers and suppliers. If you have the resources, you can get a toll-free number which your customers can call to inquire about their orders. You should also have an official email address for customer support, as well as a physical address for your business (many people use their own home addresses, but if you don't have an office, it's possible to get a post office box). If you are incapable of handling your own customer service, you may want to hire someone to do it for you because customers don't like it when you don't respond to their queries.

Create a List of Offerings

Once everything is set up in your e-commerce site, it's time for you to create a list of the products that you are offering and to publish it on your sales page. For each product that you list, you need to have high-quality pictures, a comprehensive description of the product, and a price.

Proper pricing is crucial in e-commerce and particularly in dropshipping because it's one of the things that can make or break your business. You don't want to price your products too low because you need to make a profit. At the same time, you don't want to price it too high because customers have the ability to compare your prices with those of your competitors, and they will most certainly opt to buy the product from someone else if you don't offer them a good deal. When you set your price, ensure that you factor in whatever you have to pay your supplier, plus the cost of shipping, then give yourself a decent profit margin that still allows you to stay competitive.

When you list your products on your site, you have to remember to include all terms and conditions of your service, especially terms that are related to shipping, return policies, liability in case of damages, etc.

Buy the Product from the Supplier Whenever You Make a Sale

After listing products, you may start getting sales almost immediately. When a customer makes a purchase, you need to also make a corresponding purchase from the supplier and to list the customer's address as the destination of the shipment. The customer will place his order with you and pay you immediately. You will then use that customer's money to place the exact same order with the supplier. The supplier will send out the package to your customer, and he will provide you with the shipping information, including the tracking number. You will be able to go online and see where the package is at any given time, and how soon it's expected to reach the customer. You can then notify your customer about the progress of the shipment, either by calling him or by sending him an email message. You can set up an automatic notification system on your e-commerce website for this purpose.

Also, you have to make sure that the supplier doesn't include his own personal information on the package, and he doesn't enclose receipts with his logo within the package. It's not in your best interest to let your customers know that they are actually being served by a third party instead of the business that they are actually paying.

Find Ways to Market Your Business

Finally, as you start your business, you need to come up with ways to market it. You can always use mailing lists, social media adverts, influencer endorsements, blog content, Google AdWords, internet videos, sponsored adverts, and many other internet marketing techniques to increase your visibility, distinguish yourself from competitors, and to drive sales.

CHAPTER 5 –

NICHE AND PRODUCT SELECTION

Niche selection is the first step when setting up a dropshipping business and for a lot of good reasons. The question that many people tend to ask is, does one necessarily have to identify a niche prior to setting up a dropshipping operation?

Some might argue that niches aren't necessary because dropshipping is a low-risk business, and you can just try out whatever product you want and switch to a different product if you don't find the first one to be that profitable. The truth is that there are several great reasons why it's important to choose the right product niche before you can fully set up your dropshipping business and start making sales.

For starters, having a specific niche makes it easier for you to create a brand and to market your products. Without a niche, it would be practically impossible for you to drive any traffic to your site through SEO, and even if you wanted to advertise, you wouldn't know where to begin when looking for keywords.

Having a niche makes it possible for you to strategize on things like marketing, pricing, and content creation. Niche selection also helps you identify products that can bring you real profits so that you don't have to waste time and other valuable resources doing guesswork or using trial and error to figure out where to invest.

It also helps you save a lot of money when it comes to making deals with suppliers (some suppliers may need you to pay subscription fees before they serve you, so if all your products are from different niches, you may have to spend a lot of money paying many different suppliers and distributors). Niche selection keeps you organized, and it focuses your efforts towards specific areas, so it increases your chances of succeeding in the dropshipping business.

Now that you understand the importance of niche and product selection, here are some tips to help you find the right niche for your dropshipping business:

Know the Difference Between Trending and Evergreen Niches

Before you go about selecting a niche, you should know there are 2 general types of niches—there are those that are evergreen, then there are others that are trending niches. The difference is that evergreen niches are those that remain profitable over long periods of time while trending niches are those that make large volumes of sales within a short period of time, then their sales decline. Trending niches come about as a result of hype over new products, or a sudden surge in consumer interest in a product that has already been in the market for a while.

There are some drop-shippers who chose to chase trending niches and fads, and they have been known to make sizable profits out of this practice. However, if you choose to invest in a trending niche you have to be very careful. First, you have to ensure that you join in on the fad at the correct time. That means that you enter early enough when people are still excited about the product so that you can make a profit off of it before there is a decline in consumer interest.

Second, you have to avoid getting in on trending niches way too early before you are able to tell for certain that they are actually going to trend. Some people have wasted their resources investing in niches that showed early signs of turning into fads, only for those niches to "choke" and fail to become full-fledged trends.

If you are new to the dropshipping game, and if you want to make a consistent profit over a long period of time, your best bet is to find a niche that is evergreen, or even one that has occasional trending products, but it still maintains high sales volumes when the trend declines.

Finding a Niche Using Google Trends

Google Trends is one of the best tools out there that you can use to find good niches because it can give you valuable insights into people's interest in all sorts of products. Google is the biggest search engine in the world, so it has data on a very large pool of prospective consumers.

You can use Google trends to find out what the popular product searches are at any given moment, how people's search volumes for certain products and niches have changed over long periods of time, the geographical information of people who are looking for certain products, and if people are interested in certain products throughout the year, or the changes in interest are cyclical or seasonal in nature. You can use these data points from Google Trends to identify products that are on high demand and niches that people seem interested in so that you can decide whether to invest in them.

Finding a Niche Using Facebook

You can find out if a niche that you are considering investing in is viable by using Facebook. You can type search terms related to that niche into Facebook, then go into the "groups" section of the results. When you go to "groups" you will find a list of all Facebook groups that have the search term you are looking for in their names, and you will be able to see how many members are in each of those groups.

Different marketing experts have different criteria for determining exactly how promising a niche is based on a Facebook search. Some experts claim that if a search term related to a niche yields more than 15 groups, with 30,000 or more members in each group, then it's highly likely that you are dealing with a niche that is potentially lucrative. If you are trying to narrow down from a list of possible niches to go with, it's wise to choose the niche that has the highest number of groups and members on Facebook.

Finding a Niche Using Trend Hunter

Trend Hunter is often used to find popular products within specific niches, and it can be used to assess the viability of a niche when you are trying to set up a dropshipping company. It's particularly useful when you are interested in niches where products often go in and out of fashion, or they are frequently updated. It's also a great place to find niche ideas because it lists thousands of products, all of which are meticulously grouped into categories and subcategories.

If you are considering selling a particular product, and you are looking to expand your product list based on how closely other secondary products are related to your original product of choice, Trend Hunter is the perfect place to find products that may compliment your core product. It's also the place to go when you are interested in identifying products that you can vertically integrate with your current ones in order to increase your market share within a given niche.

Finding a Niche Using Instagram

It's always a great idea to find niches that can be promoted on social media platforms, so there is an inherent advantage that comes with using Instagram as a resource for your niche research. Services such as Websta can be used to analyze statistics from Instagram. If you type your niche keyword into the search function on Websta and other similar websites, you will receive two distinctive results that are both useful for the purposes of your research. One result will be the list of people on Instagram who have your particular niche keywords in their account names. The other result you will receive will be the list of hashtags that are similar to your keyword. This data is useful because it tells you which niches can be marketed using hashtags that are already popular. If also tells you what niches you can select if you intend to work with popular Instagram influencers to market your products.

Finding a Niche Using AliExpress

AliExpress is by far the most popular supplier for drop-shippers who import products from China to the US and other western nations. It lists thousands of sellers from whom you can source your products, so it's a great tool if you want to identify products and to select niches that have the potential for profit. If you want to use AliExpress for niche research, you have to visit the website and check the statistics of the products that you are considering for your e-commerce shop. AliExpress uses a star rating system to measure product quality, so you can use it to filter out products that are of a poor quality when you are considering several options within the same niche.

You can run a product search on AliExpress and sort your results by quantity in order to rule out products that are in short supply or those that don't have a big enough market to warrant large manufacturing volumes. If you sort your products by numbers, you can be able to rule out niches that aren't popular. You can also see how long product suppliers have been listed on AliExpress (this tells you if the product is profitable in the long run).

The most important parameter that you ought to consider when using AliExpress for your analysis is the percentage of buyers who leave positive feedback in their review of the products that you are considering for your dropshipping business. The closer the positive feedback is to 100%, the more you know that you are dealing with a high-quality product that has reliable distributors. The information you gather from AliExpress can also help you figure out how to price your product, whether or not to expect consistent sales, and if a particular niche is suitable for promotion through advertising and other means.

Finding a Niche Using Amazon Tools

Amazon is the biggest player in e-commerce right now, so it's a great source of information when you are trying to figure out which niches you can use to generate some profit. Amazon has many categories of products, and you can use their system of categorization as a guide to finding out about rare products and niches. One of the best ways to stumble upon niches that are relatively unexplored is by looking at the Quirky and Unique as well as the Interesting Finds sections on Amazon. These are the categories where Amazon places products that don't squarely fit into some of their most explored niches, so if you study the products that are listed there, you may be able to coin a new niche that not many people have thought about already. This will give you the advantage of being one of the first people to specialize in that niche.

Other Ways to Find a Niche

In your quest to find a niche that is fairly unique and unexplored, don't limit yourself to the main resources that we have discussed in this chapter, instead, broaden your horizons and look as far and wide as you can. The deeper your research is, the more likely you are to finally stumble upon niches and products that are truly unique.

You can try to read blog posts about trending products and bestselling products in different niches. There are many marketing research firms that run blogs which provide a lot of useful and actionable information about changes in market trends and consumer habits. You can use this information to predict which niches are likely to perform well both in the near future and in the long run, and you can then decide to make one of them the basis of your dropshipping company.

You can also base your choice of a niche on things that you are passionate about. Search engine optimization is the best way to market your dropshipping business. If you are passionate about a topic that is related to a particular product or niche, you may be uniquely capable of creating SEO content that can market that niche, so it would make sense if you chose to invest in it. For this to work, you would have to write your own blog or create your own video content about the niche that you are passionate about, then you would use that content to drive traffic to your sales page.

If you want to figure out what niches you may be passionate about, go to the list of hobbies (Wikipedia maintains a long and comprehensive list.) and go down that list, trying to imagine yourself creating content that's related to any of those hobbies. If you find one that you think you might like, go online to find out if there are products that you can sell which are closely related to those hobbies (for example, if you are passionate about knitting, and you are willing to create content about it, there may be some knitting products that you could use your content to sell, and so you may have an advantage if you decided to pick "knitting products" as your niche).

Researching Your Competitors

It's not enough to identify a niche that could be profitable. You also have to study the other drop-shippers who have already gone into that niche and to find out if there is anything you can do to gain a competitive advantage against them. If you find a great niche that already has hundreds of retailers competing for customers, you can try to carve out a micro-niche within that niche so as to attract customers who are very specific about the products that they want to buy.

CHAPTER 6 –

HOW DOES THE SUPPLY CHAIN AND FULFILLMENT PROCESS WORK?

The term supply chain refers to the path that a product follows from the time its conceived in the mind of its creator, all the way through its manufacture and up until it gets into the customer's hands (if this were an e-commerce textbook, we would have to track the supply chain all the way back to the point where the raw materials for the product were sourced).

Because we are dealing with dropshipping, we will focus on the aspects of the supply chain where this particular model differs from other types of e-commerce retail models. There are three main players in the supply chain whose roles you need to fully grasp if you want to venture into dropshipping.

Manufacturers

The first player in the supply chain is the manufacturer. Usually, manufacturers create the products that you'll end up selling, but most of them don't sell their products to the public (at least not directly). The manufacturer sells his product in bulk to major retailers and wholesalers.

As a drop-shipper, you should want to buy directly from the manufacturers because this would allow you to enjoy larger profit margins. However, in many cases, this is not a viable option for you (given the nature of the dropshipping model).

Most manufacturers have minimum purchase requirements which drop-shippers by definition, wouldn't be able to meet. Manufacturers don't like selling their products one item at a time, instead, they would much rather fulfill large orders of products. As a drop-shipper, you can't keep your own stock, so you can't buy in bulk. For you, buying from a wholesaler is a much more viable option.

In rare cases, depending on the product that you are selling, you may be able to find a small-scale manufacturer who is willing to ship one product at a time (these are usually high-value products such as art pieces or handcrafted items). Even then, manufacturers who can handle shipping single product items are more likely to go to the market directly on their own rather than work with a drop-shipper.

Wholesalers or Suppliers

The second player in the chain is the wholesaler. Wholesalers are also sometimes referred to as distributors. They purchase products in bulk directly from the manufacturer. They then transport those goods into the individual markets where they are much closer to major retailers, and then they mark up the prices before selling the goods to retailers or largescale consumers (such as institutions). Wholesalers price their goods to cover all their expenses (including the cost of purchasing from the manufacturer, the cost of transportation, storage, and distribution), and also to make a sizable profit for themselves.

Some wholesalers have minimum purchasing requirements, but in most cases, they are much lower than those of the manufacturers. Most wholesalers stock products from multiple manufacturers at the same time and they tend to focus on specific industries. For example, a wholesaler who stocks shoes will have different brands of shoes in his inventory, but it's less likely that he will also have belts. Most wholesalers are strict about the "wholesaling" part of their business model, which means that they may refuse to ship single items to your customers and insist on selling bundled or bulk products to retailers.

Retailers and Dropshippers

The third player in the supply chain is the retailer. Retailers sell products directly to the end consumer (the public). If you are in the dropshipping business, this is the category that you fall under. Dropshippers purchase goods from those above them in the supply chain and then sell them to customers. Technically speaking, even manufacturers and wholesalers can be considered to be "drop-shippers" if their business models involve delivering goods to one party on behalf of another party. However, for the purposes of this book (and in most practical cases), drop-shippers are retailers like yourself.

Both manufacturers and wholesalers can act as suppliers, but in most cases, you'll have to buy your product from wholesalers. If you can find a supplier who is higher up in the chain, you will have to pay less for the product, and you will be able to enjoy a larger profit margin—this is however not an option in most niches and with most products out there, so you may have to settle for a supplier who is a bit closer to you in the supply chain.

A word of caution for those who are new to the dropshipping game and to e-commerce in general—don't source your products from a retailer. You too are a retailer for all intents and purposes, so buying from someone who sales directly to the public is a terrible idea because you won't have any profit margin to work with.

Your supplier shouldn't also be your direct competitor—if that's the case, then your business is doomed to fail. There are many retail businesses that pose as wholesalers who provide dropshipping services, so you should be very careful to avoid ending up working with such businesses. If you source your products from a retailer who masquerades as a wholesaler, your profit margin could end up being so thin to the point that there won't be much of a difference between you as a drop-shipper and say someone who does affiliate marketing.

Now that you are familiar with the various players in the supply chain, let's examine the dropshipping fulfillment process in order to understand what makes it unique, and what differentiates it from the fulfillment processes used in traditional e-commerce. For purposes of discussion, we will assume that you already have your dropshipping operation up and running. The following steps illustrate who the process will go, starting at the point when a customer places an order.

Order Placement by the Customer with Your Business

A customer will get in touch with your dropshipping business and place an order for one or more of your products. He will either get in touch with you by phone or use a checkout cart to place a purchase order on your website or sales page. You will then approve the order. If it's on the phone, you will acknowledge that you have accepted the responsibility of fulfilling that order. If it's online, the customer will see a message confirming that he or she has indeed made a purchase. Both your business and your customer will receive automatically generated notifications indicating that there is an order in place. The customer may get an email confirming his purchase, and you may get a notification (this is particularly important if your customer has placed the order over the Internet).

Make sure that you pay attention to your notifications so that you can take action immediately after receiving them. The customer's payment will be automatically received and deposited into your business account upon completion of the checkout process. The amount the customer pays will be the price listed on the website for the product, plus the cost of shipping (if it's indicated separately).

Order Placement by Your Business with the Supplier

You will use your business account to place an order with a supplier for the exact product that the customer wants. Most drop-shippers set things up in such a way that this step would only require them to forward the confirmation email that they receive when the earlier step is completed. Usually, the wholesaler will already have your business credit card information on file, and he will charge the wholesale price of the product together with the shipping and processing charges to that card. Some drop-shippers make use of sophisticated programs that allow the orders to be sent to the supplier automatically, but most start-up drop-shippers don't have the resources to do that, so they just use email to submit orders to suppliers.

The Supplier Ships the Order to the Customer

If there is no complication that arises at this stage (for example if the product is out of stock, or if the wholesaler is unable to successfully charge the card that he has on file), the wholesaler will take the product out of storage, package it as instructed, and then ship it to the customer's address.

The wholesaler won't print his business name or address on the package. Instead, he will print your logo, business name, address, and other contact information. The invoice that is sent to the customer along with the package will also contain your logo and letterhead, not that of the wholesaler's. When the wholesaler sends out the package, he will email you a copy of the invoice for that particular shipment, as well as the tracking information for the package.

Quality suppliers will have decent turnaround time—they may be able to ship out the order just a few hours after they receive the request. Same day shipping is a big selling point in e-commerce, so you should try to find a supplier who guarantees it.

Alert the Customer About the Shipment

When you receive the shipping information from the supplier, take note of the tracking number for the package and any other essential information, and then send it to the customer. You can send the tracking info via an email system that is built into your e-commerce site. Once the customer has the tracking information, the fulfillment process would be complete. All that is left is for you to wait and see if the customer has any complaints (e.g. if there are delays in shipment, if there is a mix-up with the product, or if the product has been damaged during transportation).

There are a few conditions that must be met in order for a dropshipping fulfillment process to work correctly. One of the most important conditions is that the wholesaler or supplier should remain invisible to the customer. Under no circumstances should the customer be aware of the fact that the fulfillment of his or her order involves another party other than you. If the wholesaler is revealed to the customer, the whole dropshipping charade will fall apart.

If the customer has a problem with the package that is delivered, he is supposed to get in contact with you and log his complaint. You will then turn around and relay that complaint to your supplier. Your supplier will take action to solve the problem, and then he will tell you what he has done, and how soon he expects the issue will be fixed. You will then call the customer and tell him exactly what the supplier has told you, but without making it sound like its someone outside your business that's actually handling the problem.

The system is cumbersome, but it's necessary for the dropshipping business model to work. If the customer finds out about your supplier, he might either lose trust in you, or he might decide to cut you out of the process and order directly from your supplier during future purchases.

So, now that you understand the structure of the supply chain as well as how the fulfillment process works, what actions can you take to ensure that the fulfillment process for your dropshipping business runs like a well-oiled machine? Well, there are a few actions that you can take to increase the efficiency of your process.

For starters, you can try to automate most of the steps that have to be taken in the order fulfillment process. For instance, you can make sure that it's very easy for your customer to place an order with you. Set up your e-commerce website in an intuitive manner and reduce the number of clicks that are needed to make a purchase.

Make sure that the payment system for customers is straightforward. When the order comes into your business, make sure that there are automatic notification systems for both you and your customer. You can also set up your system so that orders that come in from customers can go out directly to the supplier without you having to manually forward them. This will reduce the amount of effort that you have to put in, and it will reduce the chances of you failing to submit orders to suppliers because of mix-ups or human error.

You should also make sure that the card that you have on file with your supplier has adequate balance to cover the cost of the orders that you are forwarding to him. If the supplier is unable to bill you for an order, he won't have any reason to fulfill it.

CHAPTER 7 –

HOW TO FIND MANUFACTURERS AND SUPPLIERS

There are many online tools that you can use in your research to identify high quality and reliable suppliers. Let's dive right in and discuss some of those tools and how to use them properly:

Using Oberlo (oberlo.com)

Oberlo is a platform that allows drop-shippers to simply import products from different suppliers into their e-commerce shops, and then, when the customer makes a purchase, they handle all the shipping and make timely delivery of the package to the customer's address. Oberlo is fully automated, and it allows you to customize your products. This makes it a great option for those who are looking to make money off dropshipping with the least possible effort.

This site can connect your business to many suppliers around the globe, and you can scour through a large variety of products to choose the ones that you want for your store. The site also helps with product quality assurance because it has high standards for the suppliers in its catalogs.

The one downside of this site is that thousands of other drop-shippers already use it to find suppliers, so if you pick a niche or specific product based on your analysis of this site, you can be certain that you will face stiff competition in the market because other drop-shippers are doing the same exact thing. That aside, Oberlo is one of the best one-stop sites for reliable suppliers.

Run a Targeted Google Search

Being the biggest search engine, Google is always a great place to find suppliers and manufacturers, but you have to be strategic about how you run your searches if you want to find decent dropshipping partners. The first thing you need to remember here is that your search has to be absolutely extensive. The best wholesalers typically don't spend time on the internet trying to optimize their search engine visibility because they are comfortable selling to a handful of big retailers.

Most manufacturers are comfortable with being anonymous to the public, and only being known by a few wholesalers. That means that when you run a Google search for suppliers of your product of choice, wholesalers may not even pop up among the first few pages of search results. You will have to keep going on through the result, and your first decent prospect could even be located past the 50th page of the search results.

As we've said, wholesalers and manufacturers don't typically care about SEO, so when you are assessing one, don't make judgments based on the quality of their website. You could find a great wholesaler who has a website that looks like its straight out of the 90s. If you find a poor-quality website during your search, don't write it off as a scam. Instead, follow up by calling the wholesaler to find out if it's legitimate.

Also, if you are unable to find any good prospective wholesalers using your initial search terms, try to modify those terms and use ones that are somewhat similar. For instance, you could replace the word "wholesaler" with words like "distributor," "supplier," "reseller," "warehouse," and "bulk." You should also remove qualifiers from your search terms and only type in the most essential words into your search box.

Use Online Directories

There are several supplier directories that you can use as a dropshipper. The downside of these directories is that you have to pay to use them. They are massive databases that list suppliers from all product categories and niches, and they are maintained by companies that are out to make a profit by charging other businesses for that valuable information. Directories can save you a lot of time because you don't have to go through a lot of irrelevant search results. They also have their own screening processes and rules which help to ensure that they only list legitimate wholesalers.

If you can't shoulder the expense of signing up for a membership with a directory, you should just stick with using Google because, at the end of the day, you may get the same results. However, if you want the convenience of using a directory, you may be able to just sign up long enough for you to get the information that you want. Once you have noted down all the manufacturers and wholesalers that you are interested in, you can then cancel your membership to avoid recurring payments.

There are so many directories that you can use, but we will only mention some of the most popular ones that experienced drop-shippers seem to prefer.

SaleHoo is one such directory. It lists close to 10,000 suppliers, and it is currently being used by lots of merchants on sites like eBay and Amazon. Its annual fee is fairly low, and it offers 2-month money back guarantee, so you may be able to use it to find the information that you want and then cancel your subscription to get your money back.

Worldwide Brands is probably the best-known supplier directory, and it has been around since the late 1990s. It has strict guidelines for the suppliers that it lists, so you can be assured that you are dealing with legitimate and high-quality wholesalers. The downside of Worldwide Brands is that it requires a lifetime membership fee of around $300 if you want to use their services. However, if you are friendly with a lot of business owners in your area, you may find one who is a member of the site and ask him if he is willing to let you use his account to run your search.

Doba is also a well-known supplier directory, but instead of listing all suppliers, its database is limited to those who specialize in dropshipping. Even though it has fewer listed suppliers compared to other directories, it may still be a better option than most because its services are integrated with drop-shippers to allow users to place orders with several wholesalers at the same time. Because of its unique additional features (including dropshipper integration and tools that automate item listings on several marketplaces), Doba is more expensive than other popular directories—it charges its users a $60 monthly fee.

If you don't have the cash to pay for access to a directory, you can try Wholesale Central. This directory is absolutely free for users, but it charges suppliers a fee if they want to get listed or to place adverts on their website. When using this site, you need to be a bit careful because they don't have same strict screening standards as the other directories that you have to pay for (as long as a supplier is willing to pay to get listed, it's unlikely that they would turn him away even if he has serious shortcomings). In fact, irrespective of what registry you are using in your search for suppliers and manufacturers, it's still up to you to do your own due diligence to ensure that you select a supplier who satisfies all your conditions.

Go to Trade Shows

You can attend industry-specific trade shows to meet manufacturers and wholesalers within the niches that you are interested in. Trade shows allow you to network with manufacturers, to see how various products work, and to find out about new trends in your niche before everyone else gets wind of it. However, if you haven't yet settled on a niche or decided what kind of products you want to invest in, you may end up wasting a lot of time and money going from trade show to trade show.

Spy on Your Competitors

If you are entering into a niche that already has several successful drop-shippers in it, you may be able to find suppliers and manufacturers by straight up spying on the competition. You can find a major drop-shipper in a niche, and then order a small item from his shop. Once you receive that item, try to call the number on the package to find out who is on the other end. In some cases, you may find that it's the supplier who answers and not the business owner. You can then try and convince that supplier to work with you —most suppliers don't have reservations about providing dropshipping services for multiple businesses that are in competition with each other.

Contact Manufacturer to Find Distributors

If you get a manufacturer's name through any of the processes that we have discussed above and that manufacturer doesn't sell to dropshipping retailers, you can still use them to find distributors. Just call the manufacturer, identify yourself as a retailer, and ask them to send you a list of their distributor—most of them won't hesitate to comply. Be careful in your approach, because if they don't believe that you are a retailer, they might think that you are a rival manufacturer who is trying to poach their distributors, and they might then deny you access to their list.

Domestic Supplier vs International Suppliers

You may have to choose between a domestic supplier and an international one at some point in your dropshipping business. Both domestic and international suppliers have their own advantages and disadvantages, which you need to fully consider in the context of your business before you decide which option is the best for you.

Domestic suppliers are those whose operations are set up within the country. That means that if you work with them, you will be dealing with a shorter supply chain, which in turn means that you will enjoy quick delivery times.

Quality control is also more manageable when dealing with domestic suppliers because you can visit their facilities to see how they do things. Since you are within the same time zones (or within time zones that are fairly close), domestic suppliers will have a faster response time in case there are any problems that need to be dealt with. Your products will be cheaper, and you will enjoy bigger profit margins because you don't have to consider import tariffs. Also, your brand will gain more traction among consumers because you are selling products that are locally sourced.

The downside of domestic suppliers is that they are few and far between, and because they are local, the market will already be saturated with their products by the time you get into the business.

International suppliers have their own advantages as well. They provide products that aren't available locally so there is a high market demand for them. They also provide a large variety of products, and their items are generally cheaper because manufacturing costs are so much lower in other countries.

There are several downsides to using international suppliers, and most of them stem from the fact that they are located far away. Because of the distance, shipping is costlier, and you have to deal with import duties and a lot of middlemen who are all looking to get paid.

You may experience slow response times when issues arise because of the time differences as well as the language and cultural barriers. International calls are also expensive, so it would cost more to address shipment errors. Quality control is almost impossible because it would cost too much to travel to the supplier's business location. Also, some international manufacturers don't care about intellectual property laws, and you may end up in legal jeopardy if you dropship products that violate intellectual property protections. As long as you understand these disadvantages and you put plans in place to mitigate against them, you are good to go if you want to work with an international supplier.

What to Look for in a Good Supplier

In the dropshipping business, you expect to have a long and mutually beneficial relationship with your supplier, so make sure that you pick one with whom you have great chemistry. That means that you need a supplier whose staff is always professional and knowledgeable in matters that are related to your specific niche. You should be able to call them for information if you have questions about the product. Your supplier should also be well staffed. As a valued partner, they should assign you a dedicated sales representative who will be responsible for handling your account with them. This will help ensure that your problems are dealt with promptly, and when you log a complaint, it never gets lost among many other messages that the supplier receives on a daily basis.

You should also find suppliers who care about integrating modern technologies into their systems. Technology helps to further automate dropshipping businesses, and it reduces the number of tasks that you have to perform. Technology also reduces the chances of human error during the order fulfillment process. Make sure you prioritize suppliers who have real-time inventory management and detailed online catalogs. At the very least, your supplier should be able to take orders via email—calling in one order at a time is just too labor intensive, and it negates the whole reason you went into dropshipping in the first place.

Identifying Fake Wholesalers

Fake wholesalers are a real thing that new dropshipping businesses have to watch out for. There are lots of middlemen who are trying to make money from you, and unfortunately, they are the ones who invest in SEO and PPC adverts, so they often outrank legitimate wholesalers in search engine results.

There are some tell-tale signs which can bring to your attention the possibility that you are dealing with a fake wholesaler. If you find a wholesaler who is demanding that you pay a large monthly fee just so you can be allowed to make regular orders, you are probably dealing with a middleman. Real wholesalers don't need membership fees as a revenue stream because they make enough money performing their core business function, which is to buy from manufacturers and to sell to retailers at a markup. Also, beware of "wholesalers" who sell directly to the public, because they aren't really wholesalers, they are more like retailers.

CHAPTER 8 –

HOW TO OPERATE YOUR BUSINESS

If you are a novice in the dropshipping business, you could end up wasting a lot of time trying to figure out the ins and outs of running the business. To enable you to hit the ground running and to get ahead of the learning curve, let's discuss how you should operate your business once it's fully set up.

First, you have to understand that things are going to get mixed up at some point—that is the nature of the dropshipping business. The fact that most logistical functions are handled by third parties (manufacturers, wholesalers, and suppliers) means that there are lots of things that are out of your control, and so you should be mentally prepared to deal with mistakes and screw-ups.

Your suppliers will occasionally mess up your customers' orders, and sometimes, they may even run out of stock. When this happens, you may feel frustrated, and you may be tempted to give in or even to switch to a different business model. We can't lie to you and say that there won't be any challenges, but we can guarantee you that you will be able to handle most challenges if you are adequately prepared, and if you have taken the time to establish rules and protocols for all types of challenging scenarios.

One thing you need to remember is that the dropshipping model is already complicated by its very nature, so you should try as much as possible to keep things simple on your end. Try to find simple solutions to any problems that arise, rather than wasting time and resources trying to figure out the perfect solution for your problems. Things move fast in this business, and if you focus too much attention on singular events, you are going to get overwhelmed. Have a simple structure for your business, and make sure that all your operations move along smoothly.

Since mistakes are bound to happen, you shouldn't spin your wheels too much when they actually do occur. Even the best suppliers will occasionally mess up an order, and the customer will end up getting disappointed by the package he receives. Whatever the error, don't waste time passing around blame.

When addressing a customer's complaint, own up to the mistake and apologize, then take quick measures to make it up to him by seeing to it that your supplier fixes the issue. Think of every mistake as an opportunity to learn and grow.

Most professional suppliers will own up to mistakes that are genuinely theirs, so you don't have to be too confrontational when you report your customers' complaints to them. It's important to maintain a good rapport with your suppliers throughout because your success as a drop-shipper depends on it. However, if a supplier makes a habit out of messing up your orders, it may be wise to conclude your association with that supplier, because he may drag you down the path of failure.

Even though drop-shippers don't personally handle inventory, one of the biggest challenges that you will have to deal with as a drop-shipper will be the management and coordination of inventory, given the fact that you will most likely be working with multiple suppliers (we've already discussed why it's important to build redundancy into your supply system by having backup suppliers for each product in case there is a problem with your primary supplier). Managing and monitoring inventory is quite complicated, but as you gain more experience, you will become much better at it.

Even if you have a supplier and a backup supplier for a given product, you should keep a list of every other supplier who stocks the products that you are selling so that you can monitor things like price changes or the introduction of new models of the product to the market. If you don't keep tabs on all suppliers in the market, you could miss major market changes that could either render your prices unsustainable or make your products less viable. For instance, if you sell fashion accessories, your suppliers may be late to introduce new trendy items, and you would be stuck selling outdated items while your competitors cash in on the new trend.

If multiple suppliers are operating in the same niche, they may not all stock the same exact products, but chances are they all have the best-selling items in their catalogs. Always go with the supplier who offers you the best deal and don't be too hung up on loyalty—your primary aim is to increase your profit margin and make more money.

You should also exercise a lot of wisdom when selecting the products that you want to carry in your store. Try to select products that are readily available in multiple stores so that you can always have options when you have lots of order to fulfill. If you pick a product that is only available from one supplier, you run a much bigger risk of failing to fulfill an order if your supplier runs out of stock because there are no other sources of that product.

You should use generic product descriptions on your sales pages if you want to be able to fulfill orders using products from multiple suppliers. You may find that suppliers have products that perform the same exact function, but they have slight differences. For example, if you are selling accessories such as third-party chargers, they may be meant for use with the same exact phone, but they could differ slightly when it comes to aspects such as cord length, brand, color, or shape. When you list a product of this nature in your website, don't be too specific in your description because you want to have some wiggle room in case you have to fulfill customers' orders with items that have slight variations.

If the brand of a product is not well known, and it doesn't hold any value in the mind of the customer, don't constrain yourself by listing that name in your description. Instead, list the brand as "generic" because this will give you some flexibility if you found a cheaper version of the same product later on.

When you choose the products that you want to list, you should dig deep and find out if they are always available. You may find a great product, list it, and start selling it, only to discover later that it is only available for a few weeks or months, or that the manufacturer discontinued its production. Most suppliers will keep availability records for their products, so you should inquire about that. Some products could only be available during specific seasons, while others could be in shorter supply than you expected.

Knowing about a product's availability could give you an insight on how to properly market it. If a product has limited availability and you still feel like you could make some profit out of it, you could market it as a 'limited edition' product. However, if you are not very experienced as a drop-shipper, we recommend sticking with products that have high availability rates.

Even if you plan properly, you may still find that all your suppliers are out of stock at the same time and that there is no way for you to fulfill a specific order. When that happens, you should try to find a similar but slightly superior product and use it to replace the one that is out of stock. If customers have already ordered the old product, offer to upgrade their orders to the new and better one, but don't charge them extra. Most customers will be happy to get a better product for the price of the product they ordered. Even if you don't make a profit out of that particular sale, you should remember that it's always better to make zero profit than to turn away a customer.

If you have multiple suppliers who have your listed product in stock at the same time, how do you choose the one with whom to place your orders? Well, there are several criteria that you can use to make this decision. One option is to always go with your favorite supplier. This will be the one who has always been the most reliable, the one who offers the best customer service or the one with the most affordable prices. In that case, that would be your primary suppliers, and the others will be backups.

You can assign orders based on the availability of the product in each supplier's inventory. For each product that you are selling, find out which one of your suppliers has the highest amount of inventory, and then choose them as your primary supplier for that particular product. Figuring that out can be tedious if you are doing it manually, but there are services like eCommHub that can help you automate the process.

Another option is to assign orders to different suppliers based on their geographical locations. When the customer puts in an order, you will have to find out which one of your suppliers is closest to where that customer lives, and then assign the order to that supplier. There are two benefits of using this criterion—it can reduce the time taken to deliver the product to the customer, and it can also help you cut down on shipping costs.

You can also assign orders to suppliers based on the prices that they offer for each item on your store. Even if the prices from the suppliers vary by only a few cents per item, you should consider taking advantage of that because small price margins tend to add up especially if you are dealing with consumer products that sell in high volumes. When you are allocating orders to suppliers based on price, make sure that it's the total price of the sale that you are considering (that means listed price plus shipping price and any other charges that may apply).

Of all those methods, there is none that is inherently better than the rest, so select the one that you find suits you best or the one that is easiest for you to implement.

When operating a dropshipping business, you should be very much concerned with security and fraud issues because you will be handling a lot of credit card data from customers. Many merchants have found that storing their customers' credit card info simplifies things when customers want to make more purchases in the future. However, the problem with storing people's credit card information is that it's very risky, and you could end up being liable in case that information gets hacked.

For you to be allowed to store your customers' card information, you will have to comply with rules from regulatory institutions and you would have to foot the bill for expensive compliance audits. For this reason, it's much easier for you not to store customers' credit card information. Instead, if you want repeat customers, it's cheaper to invest more in marketing and scaling. If you run your dropshipping store on a platform instead of doing it on your own website, you may be allowed to store customer credit card data because most platforms are already compliant with industry regulations.

You should also be concerned about scammers posing as customers in an attempt to defraud you, or those who use stolen credit card information to make purchases from your store. There are ways to tell if an order that you have received is a fraudulent one. For example, if a customer seems to have different billing and shipping addresses, there is a high probability that he could be a scammer.

Roughly 95% of all fraudulent purchases are done by customers with different billing and shipping addresses, so make sure you take a closer look at such purchases. If it turns out that the names on the two addresses are also different, the possibility could even be much higher. However, there is always a chance that you are dealing with a gift purchase, so don't jump to conclusions.

You should also take a closer look at purchases that are made through email addresses that bear no resemblance to the customer's name (or to a real name for that matter). If the email address is formed from a random string of letters instead of sensible sounding names or words, it could be a fraudulent purchase made by a hasty scammer or even a robot.

You should also take a closer look at purchase orders that require expedited shipping. Fraudsters who charge their purchases on stolen cards may either want the purchase to be delivered fast before the real owner cancels the card or maybe they just don't care if they use the most expensive delivery method since it's not their money anyway.

To prevent fraud, you can use AVS (Address Verification System). This is a system that obligates customers to enter the address that you have on file along with the credit card number before their transaction can go through. This method has been known to significantly reduce cases of fraud in the e-commerce websites that implement it.

CHAPTER 9 –

DEALING WITH PRODUCT RETURNS AND CUSTOMER SERVICE

In dropshipping, dealing with product returns is very complicated given the fact that you don't handle the products on your own. Product returns are also very delicate situations because you don't want to sour your relationship with either your supplier or your customer, so you need to tread carefully. Here is what you need to do to ensure that you provide great customer service as you handle your product returns, and as you deal with other disputes that may arise in your dropshipping business:

Ensure You Understand Your Supplier's Return Policy

For every supplier that you work with, ensure that you have a full understanding of their return policies. Don't wait until a customer sends a product back before you start figuring out how the policy works. Every supplier has its own unique set of rules when it comes to handling returned packages. Your own return policies must reflect those of your suppliers because you can't promise something that your suppliers can't deliver.

You need to figure out if your suppliers charge restocks fees and exactly how much those charges are. You also have to find out the length of the grace period that your supplier gives customers who wish to return their packages. Additionally, make sure that you know if the customer has to cover the shipping fee for returned packages. Finally, you need to know if the supplier accepts returns of orders which result from minor mistakes made by customers. For example, if a customer orders the wrong size of a piece of clothing, can he or she then return it and change it for the right one?

You should make sure that you understand exactly how the supplier handles the whole return process in general. Is he the kind of supplier who tries to wiggle out of the responsibility of replacing spoiled items? Does the supplier have the habit of taking customers through a complicated dispute resolution process that is unnecessarily long? If you can, try to find suppliers who have return policies that are very clear, and those who have a reputation for handling returns in a gracious manner, because if they mishandle product returns, the customer will blame it on your, and this will reflect poorly on your business.

How to Create Your Own Product Return Policy

You can only create a product return policy of your own after you fully understand how all your suppliers are going to handle your customers' returns. The challenge here is to craft a single policy that accommodates the requirements of multiple suppliers who may have policies that differ. If you set up your business without clarifying your return policy, you may have a difficult time-solving clients' disputes because you will have no common frame of reference.

If you reject a customer's request for refund in a case where you don't have a written policy that explicitly invalidates his claim, the best-case scenario is that you will receive a terrible review, and the worst-case scenario is that you could get sued (especially if the product involved is of a high value).

Your return policy should match your suppliers' return policy. That doesn't mean that you should copy-paste a supplier's policy into your website and call it your own. You have to use each supplier's policy as a framework to create your own. With every condition of your policy, make sure that you stay within the constraints that have been set by your supplier. For example, if your supplier allows a 28-day return window, you could set yours at 21 days so that customers don't get punished by the supplier for issues such as shipping delays (if that happens, you may be forced to compensate the customer out of your own pocket).

Since you have to create a uniform policy, make sure that you accommodate the constraints of all your suppliers in the final draft of the policy that you create. For instance, if you have 3 suppliers, who have 28, 21, and 15-day return windows respectively, the return window that you set for yourself should be smaller than 15 days because that's the only way to accommodate all your suppliers in the same policy.

Alternatively, if you believe that a uniform return policy could hurt your sales of some items (this could happen if you give a small return window to a customer who is ordering a bulky item that would naturally take longer to ship), you could opt to create a tiered return window system where each item in your sales page gets categorized in a specific return window bracket. You could also include a summarized return policy on the sales page of each individual item.

Also, remember that you need to avoid putting a return address on your policy page because you don't want your customer sending back an item to a supplier without your knowledge. If you have multiple suppliers' addresses in your policy page, the customer might end up sending an item back to the wrong supplier because of a mix-up. If you care about customer service and product quality control, leave your own contact information in the return policy section and have the customer call you in case they have a problem with the shipment.

When the customers call, you have to ask them to ship the product to you, and not to the supplier. That's because as far as the customer knows, they are doing business with you. When you receive the package, you have to inspect it to see if the customer's complaint is a valid one and then decide what action to take. You want to act as fast as possible because the return window is getting smaller with each passing day.

Having the package sent to you instead of the supplier will also help you keep your supplier honest. A supplier may lie and say that a returned package was in good condition to get out of having to compensate you, so you have to personally verify that what the customer is saying is true.

You should never accept a return that doesn't come with a tracking number. Some customers have been known to run scams where they claim to be sending packages back, and when the package doesn't arrive, they say that it might have gotten lost in the mail, and they insist on getting compensated. Make sure that your policy clearly states that packages without tracking numbers are unacceptable and that you are not liable for them.

How to Handle the Return Process

Market surveys have shown that most consumers want to get free return shipping, and they prefer merchants who have easy and convenient return processes. Most consumers also prefer to have the return address printed right on top of the package for convenience, or they want your website to have an easy to print, premade return label. As a drop-shipper, you may not be able to meet all the conditions that your customers want you to because of the constraints of the dropshipping model, but you can try as much as possible to accommodate most of their concerns within your policy framework, and in the manner in which you process the returns.

Lots of customers end up returning packages because they ordered the wrong item. For example, it's easy for customers to order pieces of clothing that are either too small or too big. In such cases, most suppliers will not cover the return cost because it wasn't them that screwed up (in very rare cases, you may be able to find awesome suppliers who may choose to cover the cost).

You will be faced with the choice of whether to cover the cost of the shipment or to pass it on to the customer. This may come as a surprise, but we recommend that in this scenario, you should pay for the return cost out of your end. Because you are working with a small profit margin, to begin with, you may even lose money on that single transaction, but you shouldn't think of it along those lines. You should weigh that small loss against customer lifetime value—if you provide good service to the customer for that one time, you will make more money from them throughout the remainder of your future relationship with them.

If you refuse to cover the return cost, that will be the end of your relationship with the customer. Also, if the customer mentions in his review that you refused to cover the return cost, other customers may decide that buying from you is a risk that they are not willing to take. The customer should, however, take responsibility for his mistake by paying for shipping.

A customer may also return a package when the item he receives doesn't match the description that you provided for your product. In this case, the customer has absolutely no fault. If someone messed things up, it's either you or your supplier. If you created the product listing, it's on you. If you copied the supplier's product listing, it's on the supplier. If a customer returns a product under these conditions, you should be glad that he did so, because he has essentially brought a serious problem to your attention. You should immediately suspend that particular product from your store until you correct the errors in the description, or until the supplier fixes the mismatch.

Whether it's your fault or it's the supplier's fault, you have to take responsibility for the mistake and do everything necessary to promptly fix the customer's problem. Apologize to the customer, cover all the costs and find the product that the customer wanted in the first place and send it to him via priority mail. If it's the supplier's fault, you should work with him to solve the problem in a professional manner and to prevent it from happening again. However, if the supplier keeps making a repeated mistake, you may need to find a different supplier because such mistakes can be costly in the long run.

Occasionally, customers may return items that are defective or those that were damaged in transit. This occurrence should be very rare if you have a decent supplier. In this case, you should cover all the customers' costs and make it as easy as possible for them to send back the package. Afterward, you may send the package back to the supplier and ask to be compensated as well. You should also be keen on coming up with ways to prevent a repeat occurrence.

Whenever you are dealing with a product return, don't focus too much on the problem or on whose fault it is. Instead, you should focus on finding a fast and fair solution. Most customers don't really care about who is at fault. All they care about is whether their item will be replaced, or whether they will get their money back. Your formulae for dealing with returns should be simple—take responsibility and apologize to the customer, tell the customer how you intend to fix the problem, the take action to fix the problem as fast as possible. That is good customer service.

If the cost of an item is less than the shipping cost, it's definitely not worth paying to have it returned. For instance, if your customer received an older model of a phone charger instead of the newer model that he ordered, it's not worth it to anyone to have it shipped back. You can simply let the customer keep that first charger, and then send them the model that they wanted. They'll reward your generous spirit by being loyal customers from that point onwards.

In Summary, the Return Process Should Be as Follows:

The customer will make a return request. You will consider the reason for the return and see if it's valid. You will then contact the supplier and request authorization to return the package (this authorization will come in form of a unique number). You will also ask for either a refund or a replacement for that order. You will contact the customer, issue an apology, provide him with the unique authorization number, and a return address (either yours or the supplier's).

You will remind the customer to acquire a tracking number when he ships the package. When the package gets to you, you will analyze it and document any problems by taking photos. You will ship the package to the supplier. If the package goes directly from the customer to the supplier, ensure that you personally track it and that you keep tabs with the supplier.

When the supplier receives the package, he will initiate a refund or a replacement. You will ensure that your customer receives what was promised (whether it's a replacement or a refund). Throughout the process, you will work hard to be polite and friendly with both your supplier and your customer, no matter whose fault the whole thing is.

Great customer service is about taking responsibility for everything that goes wrong with your business and acting quickly to resolve all kinds of disputes. Passing blame around is no use to anyone. When dealing with customers, you should go out of your way to show them respect, and you should be patient with them if they are having a difficult time understanding how your process works. You should go the extra mile to keep your customers happy, even if they are partly at fault for whatever it is that happened that's making them return the package.

CHAPTER 10 –

HOW TO SCALE YOUR BUSINESS

The continued success of your dropshipping enterprise will depend on how well you can sustainably scale it up. The assumption among many novice drop-shippers is that they will set up their business and then the sales will start flowing in without them having to put much effort into scaling up the business. This misconception is popular because there are many people out there claiming to be dropshipping "gurus" who promise heaven and earth to impressionable entrepreneurs. Scaling a dropshipping business requires extensive investment in product research and marketing.

The truth is that if you want your dropshipping business to succeed, you need to use a hands-on approach, and you need to pay attention to all success metrics in order to figure out how you can scale it up and maximize your profits. In this chapter, we will discuss how to scale your business and increase your profitability using the best marketing strategies out there.

Here are some of the things that you should be doing on a day to day basis if you want to grow your business and win out against the competition:

Run Adverts on Social Media

Social media platforms like Facebook have billions of users, and they offer a great chance for you to reach a large audience if you want to promote your dropshipping business. If you have the capital, you should run adverts on Facebook to gain more customers. Facebook has sophisticated algorithms that allow them to collect a lot of really useful consumer data, which makes them particularly good at targeted advertising. As a dropshipping entrepreneur, you can be assured that your resources won't go to waste if you put some of them into buying niche-specific adverts on Facebook.

Another advantage of using social media adverts is that they are very customizable, and they can be adjusted to suit different budgets to target different audiences or to achieve different outcomes. If you are advertising in the Facebook ecosystem, you have the ability to make adverts of different media formats, and you can post them on different sites, including Messenger and Instagram. Facebook also has analytical tools that allow you to gauge the effectiveness of your ad campaigns.

Video content costs more to create than other types of content, but it's also the most effective when it comes to targeted advertising on social media and other Internet-based platforms. Video content is more memorable than text, so customers are more likely to remember a short video where you highlight the qualities of your product or brand, than a blog article that pretty much does the same thing.

As you make sales, add your customers to a mailing list, and you can then target them with adverts of new products. Facebook has a Custom Audiences feature that allows you to send targeted ads to people in your mailing list.

Cultivate Customer Trust in Your Business

As a business owner, one of your most important responsibilities is to get customers to trust you. This is not easy in dropshipping because customers tend to scroll fast through product listings from multiple merchants, and they may not have the time to really think about what your brand means to them. However, despite this challenge, it's still possible to cultivate customer trust by injecting more transparency into your business. On your e-commerce website, you should add features that allow customers to review your products, rate them based on quality, and provide testimonials.

Online shoppers generally don't get to see or to use the products that they are buying before they part with their cash, so they rely on the objective opinions of other consumers to help them make purchase decisions. That is why everyone pays attention to star ratings on places such as Amazon and Yelp. If you have never used a product before (or if you have never been served by a certain business before), you want to be able to benefit from the experiences of others.

If customers visit your site and they don't see any reviews, ratings or testimonials, they are more likely to give in to their doubts about the quality of your products or the reliability of your services. You should, therefore, make it as easy as possible for your customers to leave a review after purchasing and using your products. When you introduce a new product in your store and you make a few sells, you can ask some of your first customers to create text or video testimonials to help sell the product (offer them a discount or some other form of incentive if that helps).

If you source your product from a well-organized supplier, you can check to see if there are any reviews or testimonials on the supplier's website which you can then use on your own website. These reviews can help you attract customers for the time being while you continue to gather reviews of your own. Most website creation tools (e.g. WordPress) have add-ons which you can use to filter and add customer reviews to your website.

Retarget Customers Who Visit Your Site Without Making a Purchase

Did you know that in most e-commerce sites, only 2% of customers make a purchase on their first visit? That means that the vast majority of people who express an interest in your products will leave your page and they may fail to find their way back, even if they truly intend to purchase the product they are searching for in the future. The reason potential customers fail to come back to make purchases is that there are many dropshippers who sell the same product like yours, and it's likely that the customer will end up buying what he or she wants from one of their stores. So, how do you increase the chances of a customer coming back to your site when he is done window shopping and is ready to buy? To do that, you need to use retargeting techniques.

Big internet companies like Facebook and Google offer retargeting advertising services for merchants. Retargeting allows you to advertise your products to people who have been to your website before, as they go about surfing the Internet. Online marketing statistics show that previous visitors to your website are highly likely to click on retarget display ads, and they are 70% more likely to convert when they get to your site. Retarget ads can even be more successful when you categorize your target audience according to how long ago they visited your site, which pages they went to when they visited, and whether they made a wish list or abandoned a cart that they had already begun filling. Many businesses have experienced massive increases in sales after investing in retargeted adverts, so maybe you too could use these ads to boost your sales.

Use Social Media to Drive Traffic

Apart from buying adverts on social media, you should create free social media accounts on as many platforms as you can and actively use them to promote your dropshipping business. Social media platforms are increasingly becoming the best places to advertise all sorts of e-commerce businesses, more so where video content is involved. You can become an influencer yourself, or you can partner with popular influencers to try and increase your shop's visibility on social media and encourage people to try out your products.

Start a Blog to Drive Organic Traffic to Your Dropshipping Store

Blog marketing is a cheap way of reaching potential customers and attracting them to your e-commerce site. When you run a blog, your primary aim will be to grow your audience over time and to rank higher in search engines for keywords that are related to the products that you are selling. People tend to trust blogs that make a genuine effort to provide them with useful information, and if you establish your blog as an authority site on a topic that is related to your niche, lots of people will be willing to follow your recommendations when you suggest that they buy certain products from your sales page.

If you are passionate about topics that relate to your niche, you can write your own blog posts, but if you aren't, you can still hire people to ghostwrite blog posts for you. If you find the notion of writing your own blog overwhelming, and you don't have the resources to hire someone to do it, you can try setting simple targets for yourself. For example, you can make an effort to write one unique blog post every week. Before you know it, you will have a decent trove of content that will help improve your SEO and bring organic traffic to your dropshipping website.

Use Pop-Ups to Get Your Visitors to Subscribe

Did you know that more than half of the people who visit your website leave after only 15 seconds? That's a lot of wasted potential income. You can get more of them to stay or to subscribe to your email list using pop-ups. When visitors land on any of your pages, set it up so that a pop-up ad will appear on the screen asking them to subscribe.

Most people will immediately click on the "no thanks" button even without reading the notice, so try to grab their attention in other ways. You can offer them a chance to win a free product if they subscribe. You can use your "no thanks" button to nudge your visitors a little bit. For instance, you could set it to say "No, I do not want a free membership!" This will make most people stop for a while to consider exactly what they are passing over.

Find Online Forums Where Your Niche Is Discussed

These days, there is an internet forum for pretty much everything. If you select a niche for your dropshipping business, chances are that there are forums online where people who are interested in that niche share ideas and discuss the merits and demerits of various products. If you run an online search, you could find groups on Facebook or threads on sites like Reddit where potential customers congregate to share their interests.

You can join such groups to see what your prospective customers are talking about. This can help you in a number of ways. First of all, you may be able to target them and sell your products to them. Secondly, you may be able to find out what kinds of products they want, and this could give you a competitive advantage over other players in your niche. Thirdly, you could find out about upcoming trends in your niche, and you could be among the first to catch on to those trends.

When contributing to online forums, don't be too obvious about the fact that you are promoting your products. You could be kicked out for spamming the forum or the group. Instead, try to provide some useful insights first so as to cultivate trust before you can begin making subtle suggestions asking the other forum member to visit your site. When dealing with Facebook groups in your niche, try to find out who the group administrator is, and try to recruit him or her into helping you reach out to the members of the group. You can sweeten the deal by offering the group members exclusive product discounts or some store credit.

Use Market Analytics to Monitor Your Progress

When you are looking to scale up any business, you need to take account of all the progress you are making in order to come up with better strategies to help your business grow. The good news is that as an e-commerce retailer, you have lots of analytical tools at your disposal, which you can use to monitor traffic, to gauge the effectiveness of marketing campaign strategies and to figure out how to boost sales.

Facebook has conversion pixel data, while Google has its renowned analytics tool, so if you use either platforms for customer acquisitions, you may be able to track every conversion that you get and try to figure out what you can do to replicate it with other prospective customers. You can use these tools to find out exactly where a specific customer originated, what web pages he had to go through before ending up at your website, and what he did in your website before finally making a purchase. Using analytical tools to review data is the closest that you can get to actually reading your customers' minds and following their thought processes.

Finally, in order to successfully scale up your business, you must remember to stay current and relevant. That means that you need to update both your products and your website as often as necessary so that you don't get left behind as things change. When your supplier releases new versions of products, make sure that you are notified and that you become one of the first merchants to carry that product. If new marketing strategies emerge, or if new social platforms gain popularity, make sure that you are among the first to use them to generate traffic for your store. In the dropshipping business, if you are not quick to evolve, you will get extinct.

BONUS 1 –

HOW TO DROPSHIP WITH SHOPIFY

Shopify is by far the best online tool for drop-shippers who don't have the technical expertise to create their own shops. It makes it possible for anyone to sign up and start his own online store in just a few minutes. It's great for people who want to start a dropshipping business but lack the technical know-how or the resources to build their own e-commerce websites from scratch. If you want a hassle-free experience as you start your first store, you should seriously consider using Shopify. The service offers free trial periods for beginners who want to test the waters before making a financial commitment. Here is a step by step guide to help you start your first Shopify dropshipping store.

Choose a Name for Your Dropshipping Store

When creating a Shopify store, your first task will be to select a name for your dropshipping business. You want to make sure that the name you select is simple, creative, and memorable. If you already have a niche in mind, you could try to find a name that is related to that niche so that people can have an easy time figuring out what you are selling. There are some online business name generators that you could use to come up with a list of possible names before you narrow it down to one.

When you find a few possible names that you may want to use, you must check to see if they are available. Google each of your shortlisted business names to see if they are already in use. If you use obvious sounding names such as "American Watches," chances are someone has already thought of that, and they are already trading under that business name, so try to think outside the box.

Create a New Shopify Account

Shopify has made this step extremely easy. All you have to do is go to the Shopify homepage. At that page, you will find a field where you have to enter your email address to start the process. Once you have entered the address, click the "get started" button. You will then be asked to create a password and input your chosen store name. Shopify will ask you a few questions about how much experience you have had in the e-commerce sector, and then they will ask you to provide a few accurate personal details. After you are done providing those details, your account will be officially opened, and you can then proceed to optimize your settings.

Set Up Your Account and Add All Necessary Information

You have to go through your new account's settings one menu item at a time, and you are going to input the information you need to configure your account before it can be operational. You have to put in place the correct settings to allow you to receive customer payments, to create your shipping rates, and to establish your store policies.

When customizing your account, your first task will be to add one or more payment options to your store. Unless you have this in place, there will be no way for your customers to pay you for the products they'll purchase. Go to your Shopify settings page and click on the tab that has the word "payment" on it. You will have the option to add a PayPal account or to use other payment solutions.

We highly recommend that you use PayPal because it's extremely convenient and it has a deep market penetration, so most people who shop online already have PayPal accounts of their own. You can also opt for other payment systems if you find them convenient or necessary given the particular nature of your products (for example, if yours is a store that mostly sells products to offices and other businesses, you may find it more convenient to add a payment system that allows for bank transfers.

After you have all your payment channels in place, it's time to set your store policies. These policies will govern the relationship between you and your customers, so you should make sure that they are clearly stated and that they are compliant with the law.

Shopify understands exactly what kind of policies you might need for your store, so they have created a tool that enables you to automatically generate store policies that are standardized. You can immediately generate a refund policy, a privacy policy, and even a set of terms and conditions that will protect your store from legal liability in many foreseeable situations. To gain access to the policy creation tool, you have to click on the "checkout" tab, the go through the page to find each of the fields that you have to fill. You can then click on the "generate" button, and your policy will be set.

When your customers check out after making a purchase, the full text of the policy will appear, and they'll have to accept those terms and conditions before the sale goes through. If you have your own conditions that you want to include in the policy, there are some templates that you can use as guides to create your own policy.

Finally, you will have to declare your shipping rates. Many e-commerce experts recommend that you should account for the shipping price when you mark up the price of each item in the store, and then, you should offer your customers "free shipping." This is a marketing technique that works pretty well because it makes most customers believe that they are getting a great deal, so they'll be more inclined to go through with the purchase. You can click on the 'Shipping' button and select your preferred shipping options for different zones, starting with domestic ones and proceeding all the way to international zones.

Launch Your Dropshipping Store

After you are done with your settings and configurations, you should proceed to launch your new dropshipping store. To do this, click on the "sales channels" option, and then click on "Add sales channel." When you are done with that step, you will have a real online business that is up and running.

Design and Personalize Your Store

Now that you own an online store, it's time to personalize it. Here, you have to consider how you want your customers to view your site as they browse through it and make purchases. The design of your shop is going to be crucial, and it may have a huge bearing on your level of success as a drop-shipper. You want to make a good first impression when customers visit your site, and you want to project an image of professionalism. The two most important design aspects that you have to consider are the theme and the logo of your shop.

Shopify has a large collection of themes in their inbuilt theme store, so you don't have to worry about finding a theme that suits your brand. You can use a free theme option, or you can pay a little money for a premium theme. If you are working under a tight budget, a free theme will do just fine. However, if you are very particular about your branding, you may want to go for a premium theme. Try out a few themes before you settle on one. After selecting a theme, you can customize it to make it more reflective of your brand.

Logos are important for branding purposes because they enable customers to remember your dropshipping store in case they want to make more purchases in the future. Your logo should blend with other design aspects of your shop because you want to create a sense of uniformity.

You can use tools like the Oberlo Logo Maker to create a high-quality logo in a matter of minutes. All you have to do is play around with colors, fonts, and icons. If you are a skilled graphics designer, you can create your own logo and upload it onto your Shopify account. You can also hire graphic design experts for cheap on sites like Fiverr and Upwork. After you are done with both the logo and the design of your store, it's time to add your products.

Add Products to Your Store

To add a product to your shop, go to Shopify Admin and click on "Products." You should then click on the "Add a Product" button on the top right part of the page.

You will then have access to fields where you can enter the title and the description of your product. Fill the fields by either copying and pasting the text from your supplier's website or adding a description that you have prepared on your own. Make sure that you use colorful language in your product description because your customers are going to make purchase decisions based on that description.

You should then scroll down the page and find the "Images" section. Here, you have the option of adding images by uploading image files from your computer. You can also use "drag and drop" to achieve the same outcome. Make sure you upload your favorite product image first because it's the one that is going to act as a "featured image," meaning that it will appear prominently on the sales page when your customers scroll through your shop.

You should then review all your product details, particularly the "visibility" settings to make sure that your product is set to appear on the online store. You should also review the "Organization" settings and modify them to make sure your product is properly categorized according to Vendor, Product Type, and Collections.

You then have to input the price of the product. As you do that, you can select an option that makes it possible for customers to compare prices, and you can also check a box that allows a tax to be added to the final price of the product.

When you get to the inventory section, you should add your SKU, your Inventory Policy, and a Barcode. Indicate whether or not your product has a shipping price, then select the weight bracket of the product. If your product comes in different sizes and colors, you should fill the "Variants" section appropriately, and put in the different prices for each variant.

Finally, you should edit your Meta Title and Meta Description in order to improve your SEO (search engine optimization) so that customers will have an easier time finding your product online. Ensure that you save all your product information correctly and that you view your product listing from the front end to see it from the point of view of the customer. You should repeat all these steps to add more products, or you can use services such as Oberlo which can help you add products to your account automatically.

Start Selling and Cashing in

Now that everything is done, you can start making sales. Remember that dropshipping is a competitive business, so you should do everything that you can to promote your products on blogs, social media, and other websites. Advertising is also an option if you have the resources.

BONUS 2 –

HOW TO DROPSHIP ON AMAZON & EBAY

If instead of creating your own website, you want to dropship on an existing platform or marketplace, Amazon and eBay should be among your top considerations. Let's discuss how you can set up your dropshipping store on these two marketplaces.

Amazon

Being the biggest name in retail e-commerce, Amazon has a lot of inherent advantages as a dropshipping platform. You can open a dropshipping account with Amazon and take advantage of their market share and stellar reputation to sell your products. Amazon buys products from suppliers in bulk, so they have massive inventory in warehouses in different parts of the world, which means that if you work with them, your small shop could grow fast and operate globally.

DROPSHIPPING

With Amazon, you also have access to a large market of more than 300 million users, which means that you could get large returns if you have great products and strategies. Because Amazon already has hundreds of millions of potential customers, you don't have to spend too much on advertising. In fact, you can easily advertise within the platform itself. If you optimize your page, you could get organic traffic there without needing to advertise.

Before you choose Amazon for your dropshipping platform, you should understand that they have one major downside. They prioritize merchants who use their FBA program over those who dropship with the help of third-party suppliers. If you are using Amazon's FBA program, you actually have to buy your inventory upfront and send it to Amazon's warehouses where it will be stored until it's shipped out to customers. If you wanted to limit your startup costs to almost zero, the FBA program probably isn't your best option, so stick with dropshipping. That being said, Amazon is a great place for drop-shippers because it has some of the best shipping times and quality control measures in the whole retail e-commerce business.

Many people think that dropshipping is against Amazon's terms of service, but it's actually not. Amazon doesn't allow arbitrage dropshipping (this is where people source products that are cheaper from places like Walmart and eBay and then sell them through Amazon). Amazon allows private third-party fulfillment of customer orders, as long as it's your business name that appears on all the purchase and shipping slips that are attached to the product. According to the Amazon TOS, you have to be the "seller of record," which means that if you use a competitor of Amazon's (like Target or Walmart), they may close your account.

Here is how to go about dropshipping on Amazon:

First, you should get a professional Amazon seller account. You should pay the fee for a pro account because the free account will limit your ability to grow and scale once you have started your dropshipping business. There are also certain categories in Amazon's platform in which you cannot sell products if your account is a free one.

You also need to get UPC codes (Universal Product Codes) for all your products. There are lots of services online that can help you acquire UPC codes, so with a little internet research, you can easily figure out how that works. You also need to get suppliers, and they shouldn't be big box suppliers (big companies that compete with Amazon in the retail market).

Use a product research tool to find a great product to sell on Amazon. Remember that with Amazon, it's even much harder to compete in popular niches because there are other sellers who have been around longer and they have positive reviews, so you have to go an extra mile in your product research.

You also need enough capital to sustain your business in the first few months because it takes a while for Amazon to pay its merchants, so you can't count on the payout from your sales to maintain cash flow.

Also, make sure that your suppliers ship the products pretty fast (preferably within 5 business days). That's because Amazon customers are accustomed to fast shipping, and the platform keeps metrics of its drop-shippers which customers can see. If your metrics are poor, customers won't be too keen on buying from you. Amazon is a bit strict when it comes to quality control, and if you get a high number of product returns or cancelations, or if your metrics are terrible, they could suspend you from their platform.

As a drop-shipper on Amazon, the way you create and organize your listings will determine how many sales you will be able to make. First, to increase your chances of success, make sure that you have lots of product listings on your account. Second, you have to be well organized in the way you list your products. Make sure that you use bold and clear titles and descriptions that sound like professional sales copy. You should also use high-quality product images for all items in your listings. As a drop-shipper, you may not be able to use PPC ads for your products because Amazon prioritizes FBA merchants over drop-shippers, so your best chance of boosting your visibility is by optimizing your product pages.

You should be careful when selecting the products to dropship on Amazon because not all products are suited to be drop-shipped on this platform. You should choose a niche where people are passionate and very specific about the products, which means that they will be willing to wait a little longer to receive that particular product. If you go to a niche where products are readily available everywhere else, you may not be able to compete with merchants who use FBA, mostly because of their faster shipping times.

Most Amazon drop-shippers eventually end up switching over to the FBA program. They use dropshipping to test the viability of a product in the market, and then if it works well, they switch to FBA to take advantage of Amazon's fast shipping, advertising, and other perks. If you have the capital, you can adapt this model to increase your competitiveness within the Amazon platform. If you would rather stick with dropshipping, you may be able to offer incentives to your customers to make them more willing to wait for a little longer for their packages. You can add a small freebie to every product that your customers purchase to entice them to select your products despite the longer shipping times.

Finally, when shipping with Amazon, be extremely careful about copyright and trademark issues because you could get authenticity claims from big companies, and Amazon could shut your down. Otherwise, Amazon is a great place to run a dropshipping business, and all you have to do to succeed there is to work smart and hard and follow the rules.

eBay

eBay is a great platform for dropshipping mostly because it adds a twist to the dropshipping model. Instead of just having a fixed price for your products, you can set up auctions for each listed item (especially if the products you are selling are rare and high-value items). It's also less restrictive when it comes to the kind of products that you can sell. Unlike Amazon, you don't have to worry too much about where you source your products, as long as you are able to deliver.

eBay is like the wild west of online retail because it allows people to sell all sorts of new and used items, so if you want to stand out and gain the trust of customers, you should be able to provide as much information about yourself and your product as you can and try to make your listings look professional. Compared to other platforms where you can start your dropshipping business, eBay is probably the cheapest because it doesn't charge any fees (like Shopify and Amazon).

To start dropshipping on eBay, go to their website and open an account. You can either open a personal or a business account, that doesn't matter since most dropshipping functions can be performed by both accounts, plus you may be able to upgrade a personal account into a business one if the need arises. The account opening process is fairly standard. You just have to fill in your personal information and contact information, and towards the end of the process, you will need to add a PayPal account to your eBay account. After signing up, you can personalize your account by adding a logo. The whole process should take you less than ten minutes if you have all your details ready.

When you start selling on eBay, you will only be allowed to list a few items at a go (about 10 items). As you make more sales, the platform will increase your limit more and more. You have to write good product descriptions with eye-catching titles for your products, indicate their prices, and then use high-quality images to show the product from multiple angles. eBay listings differ slightly from listing on personal websites or other platforms because you have to add terms of sales and shipping information within the description for each product.

For each product that you list on eBay, you have to go through the same listing process since eBay doesn't support synchronized settings across multiple listings. If you exceed your listing allowance, eBay might charge you a listing fee for the extra products. eBay listings usually expire after thirty days, so if you want yours to stay up beyond that period, you have to go to 'setting details' and set your preferred duration for that listing. The "Good till canceled" option ensures that your product stays on the site until you decide otherwise.

You will then input the price, quantity of items, payment options, buyer privacy setting, sales tax for the product, and your preferred return options. When it comes to returning options, you have to choose the length of the return window for the product, and the action that you will have to take when dealing with returns. If you feel like your customers could benefit from some further explanation of your return policy, there is a field where you can insert additional information.

You will then have to fill in all your shipping details. You can select different shipping options for different regions. You should also specify your shipping method, fees, durations, etc. You will then click the "list" button to publish your listing on eBay. In case you have left an important detail out, eBay will notify you and allow you to fix the error.

After you have listed your product, you could start promoting it on social media platforms almost immediately to drive traffic to your page. When you make sells, you will contact your supplier and have him ship the product to your customer within your stipulated time period.

BONUS 3 –

MISTAKES TO AVOID WHEN STARTING THE BUSINESS

Here are some common mistakes that many novice dropshippers tend to make. We will discuss why people find themselves making these mistakes, and what you should do to avoid making them:

Starting Without Learning the Ins and Outs of Dropshipping

There has been much hype around the topic of dropshipping, and a lot of misinformation came along with it. Many self-proclaimed "dropshipping gurus" have been telling people how easy it is to start a dropshipping business, and this has led a lot of people to assume that you don't need to learn any technical aspects of the business to succeed. The truth is that the dropshipping game is evolving pretty fast, and there is stiff competition in every niche, so you should avoid jumping into the business without taking a little time to learn as much as you can about the trade.

Choosing Bad Suppliers

Many newbies fail to look into the history of suppliers to find out if they have a reputation for unreliability. They assume that in order to maximize their profits, they need to go with the supplier who offers the lowest prices, but the truth is that the quality of service and the reliability of a supplier is much more important for a drop-shipper than saving a few cents on each order. If a supplier messes up and makes a lot of excuses during your first few weeks of operation, you should drop him and find a more reliable one before your business gets stuck with a bunch of negative reviews.

Lacking Faith in the Dropshipping Model

For you to succeed as a drop-shipper, you have to stick to the model. Some first-timers make the mistake of doubting how the model works, so they try to blend dropshipping with other forms of retail e-commerce. This often happens when newbie drop-shippers worry about their suppliers running out of stock, so they go out and use their own money to buy some inventory. If you have chosen to be a drop-shipper, you should stick with it and concentrate on scaling your business, and you should avoid complicating things unnecessarily. Have faith that the system will work.

Expecting Money to Come Easily

Again, the notion that dropshipping brings in quick and easy money comes from the so-called experts who misinform people because of their own personal agendas. As a drop-shipper, don't assume that you will set up a store, launch it, then sit back and start watching the money flow in. Success in dropshipping requires hard work, proactivity, and a competitive attitude. Customers don't just come to your shop, you have to go out there on the internet, find them and bring them in through advertising and content marketing. Dropshipping is not a get rich quick scheme.

Failing to Retarget Your Site Visitors

Retargeting site visitors is probably the most effective marketing strategy out there in terms of the sales that it generates. If you don't take advantage of retargeting ads on Facebook or Google, that's akin to throwing money away. People visit a shopping site or a sales page because on some level, they really would like to buy that product, so if you keep reminding them about it, one day, as soon as they can get some money, they are highly likely to come back and make that purchase. If you have limited marketing funds, make retargeting ads a priority in your marketing strategy.

Using Low-Quality Product Images

First-time drop-shippers are encouraged to use free photos as a cost-cutting measure, but that doesn't mean that you should use low-resolution product photos. If your supplier provides low-quality photos, try to find better photos of the product elsewhere online, or you can order a sample of the product and take your own photos of it. Online shoppers don't get to see the products they are buying beforehand, so they rely on photos to make purchase decisions. To be fully convinced about the quality of a product, most of them would want to see lots of high-resolution photos from different angles so that they can zoom in and study the product in detail.

Misleading Your Customers About Your Shipping Time

Many new drop-shippers are afraid that the customer might go elsewhere if they think that the shipping time for a product is too long. Some drop-shippers are tempted to either conceal the real shipping time or to straight up lie about it. If you can't guarantee fast shipping for a certain product, you should be honest about it, and offer an explanation as to why it's taking longer than expected (perhaps you are shipping it from abroad). Misleading customers about your shipping time counts as terrible customer service, and if a customer has to wait longer for a package that he was promised, he is highly likely to take his business elsewhere.

Being Afraid to Reinvest Your Money in the Business

When dropshipping novices make a little money from their businesses at the beginning, some are usually afraid of putting the money back into the business for fear that they could end up losing it all. However, the right approach is to reinvest at least some of the money you make into the business through adverting or SEO. There are lots of ways to advertise one's dropshipping business—you could hire influencers, buy PPC ads, etc. Your business won't grow if you take every cent you make out of it. Use your proceeds to scale your business in order to make more profits.

Failing to Work with Instagram Influencers

Right now, Instagram is one of the hottest platforms if you are looking to advertise any kind of product. People follow influencers on Instagram to an almost religious extent, and you would be surprised at how many people will be willing to buy a product just because one influencer mentioned it. You can easily find an influencer within your niche who is willing to give your store or product a shout out for a bit of cash. The bigger you dream, the bigger you'll grow, so don't be afraid to spend a lump sum of cash for an endorsement from a few powerful influencers.

Using Complicated Shipping Fee Structures

First-time drop-shippers tend to publish complicated shipping fee structures on their websites or to display shipping fees under the price tag of every item in their shops. This can be confusing and off-putting for many customers. Customers don't need to see your cost breakdowns, they just want to know how much the whole thing is going to cost them. Instead of having separate shipping fees for all listed items, you should just set prices that account for shipping costs and then offer free shipping. This is a neat marketing trick that can make customers think that you are offering them a great deal.

Creating Unclear Policies

Many novice drop-shippers make the mistake of thinking that store policies are mere formalities, so they fail to make them as clear as necessary. You should avoid having unclear policies. If you don't know how to create such policies, you can borrow ideas from other similar businesses, or you can use online tools provided by industry players such as Shopify. For example, if you don't explicitly state in your policies that a customer has to include a tracking number when returning a package, and then the customer claims that he sends back the package without producing a tracking number to prove it, you won't have any recourse if the package "gets lost in the mail."

Mishandling Product Returns

Product returns are complicated and frustrating for drop-shippers because they require a lot of correspondence, and they cost money. However, they are also an opportunity for you to deliver good customer service, and they help you learn the weaknesses in your system so that you can fix them. Many first-time drop-shippers mishandle product returns by trying to shortchange the customer or by taking their frustrations out on the supplier. You have to remember that returns are part of the business and in the end, they are inevitable. You should prepare for them by outlining clear rules on how they ought to be handled and by sticking to those rules even if things get frustrating.

Relying Too Much on One Supplier

Many drop-shippers make the mistake of counting too much on a single supplier. This leaves them unprepared in case anything unexpected happens. You should always have several backup suppliers for every product in your store. If something happens, say your supplier runs out of stock or hikes up his prices, you can count on your backups to fill your orders. If you are in a situation where your business could live or die depending on the actions of a single supplier, then you are not managing your risks properly.

Failing to Test Several Products

You may have a niche in mind when you start your business, and you may select great products that bring in a decent profit, but that shouldn't be the end of it, you should keep testing new products to see if you can make money off of them. If you are inflexible about the products that you carry in your store, you could wake up one day to find that there is a universal shortage of your best-selling product, so it's good to have backup products. By testing several products, you can identify those that may come in handy when you want to scale your business.

Focusing on Price Competition

Many first-time drop-shippers make the mistake of thinking that they can beat out the competition by setting their prices lower than everyone else. While it's true that customers like bargains and low prices, there are other more sustainable ways to make your store stand out from the competition. If you start a price war, you will be digging your own grave. Whenever businesses start undercutting each other, it's the ones that have few resources that end up losing. You cannot undercut dominant online retailers because they are always willing to match the lowest price, so you have to differentiate yourself by offering great service with a personal touch.

Selling Products That Violate Trademark or Copyright Laws

Just because a supplier has a product available in his inventory doesn't mean that it is entirely legal. There are many cases where suppliers stock knockoff products that are often imported from Asia. You may also see clothes or accessories with nice logos from popular Western franchises and decide to sell them in your store. You should be extremely careful in these situations because some of those products may violate the legal rights of other businesses, and you could get sued by the companies that own the trademarks, copyrights, or other intellectual properties that were used to make those products.

CONCLUSION

Thanks for making it through to the end of *Dropshipping: A Beginner's Guide to Making Money Online*. I hope that you learned a lot of useful information that will provide you with the expertise that you need to start your own dropshipping business and succeed as a dropshipping merchant.

Your next course of action is to boldly venture into the dropshipping game and to make yourself as much money as you can. As long as you remember to apply the knowledge that you've learned in this book, you should be able to stay ahead of the competition and grow your business to its maximum potential.

One thing you need to remember is that the dropshipping landscape keeps changing every day, so you should do your best to stay informed about new trends in all facets of the business, especially when it comes to marketing and advertising. When new marketing trends come around, find out how viable they are and don't hesitate to invest in them. Even after you get to the top of the game, remember to stay proactive and don't be afraid to keep evolving.

In dropshipping, like in most other businesses, knowledge is power. So, if you are in the business for the long haul, don't ever stop reading and acquiring knowledge. Read books, blogs, and newsletters about dropshipping to stay sharp. Even if you have bestselling products in your store, you should keep researching new products because the wind might shift, and you need to be prepared.

Made in the USA
Lexington, KY
31 July 2019